SHATTERED

LESSONS IN SURVIVAL & STRENGTH:

*One woman's journey through accepting guilt,
surviving prison, and finding strength on the other side*

JESSICA RASDALL

ISBN 978-0-692-94101-0

Printed in the United States of America

Disclaimer:
The author has made every effort to ensure the accuracy of the information within this book was correct at time of publication. The author does not assume and hereby disclaims any liability to any party for any loss, damage, or disruption caused by errors or omissions, whether such errors or omissions result from accident, negligence, or any other cause.

In Loving Memory of Laura
July 29, 1987 – February 25, 2006

Thank you for giving me something bigger than myself to fight for.
I can only hope to be half the woman you would have been.
I love you, La. I am so sorry.

Table of Contents

Preface

Eleven years ago I searched for a book that would tell me how to pick up the pieces of my shattered life. I couldn't find anything. The following pages share with you my journey on a mission to "put the book on the shelf."

Each pillar (chapter) shares a part of my personal journey. At the end of each chapter, you'll find either a "What Can I Do?" or "Consider This" section. Those sections are a special part of the book with a message just for you.

Although my story may be different from your own, my hope is that the messages and action steps will resonate with you and your own story. My story is simply being used as an example on this journey we're taking, together. As you read the message at the end of each pillar, please apply the action steps to your story.

Author's Note

These pages contain a story that impacted countless lives. Please note I am only sharing my experience on that journey. Out of respect for Laura's family, their journey is not included in the narration of this story.

INTRODUCTION:
Bookstore Breakdown

There I was, in the middle of the self-help section of a Barnes and Noble bookstore. I was on the verge of a breakdown, feeling like I had reached the end of my road. I touched every book. I ran my fingers across the spines, over the titles, like the one I needed would magically appear. What to do after losing your child . . . after losing a parent . . . overcoming alcohol addiction. It looked and felt as if there were books for everybody, for every journey, for every struggle—except mine.

I had been in this same store countless times before and had always found what I was looking for. Not this time.

In this bookstore, surrounded by thousands of books, yet not one single book to help me, I felt I would never find my answer. There would never be a road map for me. If nobody knew what the next step was, if there was no book to tell me what to do next, then maybe there wasn't one. Maybe there wasn't a next step. Maybe, just maybe, I had reached the end of my road.

How could I possibly come back from this? How could I go on? Did I deserve to go on? I sat on the floor with my head down, trying to understand. I thought, *This is the end.*

An employee approached me. The young man must have seen me looking at this shelf, picking up every book, searching for something. He asked if he could help me find a book. Without hesitation, I reacted. I said, "Yeah, when you get the book titled *I Killed My Best Friend and Now I Don't Know What to Do*, I'd really like to read it. Until then, there's nothing you can do to help me."

I instantly broke down in tears. There it was: I'd hit it. There was the breakdown. After three weeks of bottling up all of my emotions, I reached my breaking point. I fell to the floor and started crying uncontrollably. I apologized, and kept saying over and over to this boy, "I'm so sorry. This is not about you."

My mother rushed over and asked, "What's wrong? What just happened?" I told her, "There's nothing here. There's nothing on the shelf to tell me what to do next. There's nothing to help me." So calm, and so serious, she responded, "Well, if there isn't anything for you on that shelf, then maybe you should put something on that shelf."

She was right. In that moment, I drew a line in the sand. I decided I was going to make it through. I was going to take that next step. I was going to draw my own map, chart my own course, write my own book. No matter what I would face ahead, I was going to make it through—even if only to show someone else that it is possible.

Permission to Chart Your Own Course

Maybe that's you right now. Maybe you can feel the breakdown coming. Maybe you've already had it. Maybe you don't even know what I'm talking about. But if you're feeling like that girl in the bookstore, if you feel like you are in life's uncharted territory, that there's no road map for what you're going through, that nobody understands, then every time somebody tells you everything happens for a reason, or it's going to be okay, you just want to scream.

I need you to know that there isn't a road map for life's uncharted territories, but you have to keep going. It's not easy. It's not always going to be one foot in front of the other. This journey is not linear at all. It's not a straight line. You don't go from point A to point B in order to get to the end. You'll have to go up, down, back, and forth. But we just have to keep moving.

I'm here with you. I'm here to help you. You don't have to do this alone.

Know that in order to move forward, you may have to leave some people behind on this journey—the ones who said you can't make it, the ones who said you're not good enough, and the ones who said you should just throw in the towel. But that's okay. You're on a new journey, and some pieces of the old journey will have to fade away. Know that there will be new people. You'll find your support system along the way: the people who believe in you, the people who want to see you succeed. Your guardian angels.

Most importantly, know that I am right here with you. I'm still in the trenches, and I'm going to go through this alongside you. These next pages won't be easy. You might uncover some things you don't want to talk about, some things you've buried. It might seem out of order or unconventional, but I need you to trust the process. Keep going, and give yourself permission to do the work. I know it can be easy to just seek forgiveness: forgiving ourselves, forgiving others who have done us wrong, forgiving past experiences. Everybody pushes us to forgive. I cannot tell you how many times people asked me, "Have you forgiven yourself yet?" like that should be the end goal.

Forgiveness doesn't have to be the only answer. Maybe surviving is enough.

So as you're going through this process, just keep going. Make that your end goal. Make your goal to simply never stop moving. Forgiveness happens along the way, but you can't force it.

Thank you for trusting me on this journey. I can't wait to see where your road map leads.

When Life Punches You in the Gut: *Now What?*

Just when we think our world is coming to an end, a new story is just beginning.

How Did I Get Here?

When I opened my eyes, the windshield, shattered and pieced together only by shreds of tinted film, was just inches from my face. I looked to my left and the driver's side window was completely gone. I could hear cars on the highway behind me flying by, but no one was stopping to help. I looked down and saw that my hands were covered with dirt, glass, and blood. There was so much blood. Where was it coming from? Where was I? That bloody Honda "H" on the steering wheel, now burned into my memory, was the only clue that I was in my car. *Where was I going? Where was I tonight? What happened? How did I end up on the side of the road?* So many questions—but no answers.

I was in fight or flight mode. One moment I was sitting there lifeless, consumed with pain, unable to move, and convinced that I was about to die, right there, trapped behind my steering wheel.

The next moment, a wave of indescribable energy took over. I tried anything and everything to get out of my car. I honked my horn for someone to help me and tried to climb out of my window. But I was stuck. And then I looked to my right. When I turned my head, I realized there was somebody in my passenger seat. I panicked. *Who is this? Who did I give a ride home?* I shook her. I grabbed her arm. "Please wake up," I begged as I screamed uncontrollably.

She didn't respond as her arm fell lifelessly down at her side.

I had no idea who she was. I didn't know how she got in my car or where we had been going. I didn't know what happened earlier that night. There was something about the way she was positioned on the seat, the way that her right foot was resting on her left knee. There was something about that position that was so familiar to me, yet I just couldn't put my finger on it. I panicked and yelled for someone to help us. "Is there someone out there? Anybody?"

A part of me knew that this person next to me wasn't alive. I panicked.

Sometimes there are moments when unexpectedly, out of left field, life punches you in the gut. She knocks the wind out of you. The only thing you can say is, "What the hell was that, and now what am I supposed to do?" Life didn't just knock the wind out of me, it knocked the life out of me.

I didn't know it then, but I would soon find out that there was so much more than glass shattered that night.

When Life Was Normal

Why is it so much easier to make friends as kids than as adults? A kid sees another kid on the playground and immediately wants to make a new friend. But as adults, we don't always want to meet new people.

I met Laura in kindergarten. We went to the same elementary and middle school, a very small school. But it was in third grade that we became inseparable. One day, over a silly classroom conversation, I asked her if she watched the show *Dawson's Creek*. When she said yes, I asked her to sleep over at my house that weekend. We became inseparable.

Weekends were filled with sleepovers, during which we would stay up late watching old, scary movies, eating way too much junk food, and giggling late into the night. She was my other half and my polar opposite. I was the short brunette; she was the tall blond. She had dirty blond hair, though, and she wanted it to be bleach blond. She wasn't allowed to color it back then. Once when she was spending the night at my house, we mixed up a concoction of hair conditioner and hydrogen peroxide, and I painted highlights into her hair with an acrylic paintbrush and wrapped it in aluminum foil. We thought we were so cool doing our own highlights.

A few weeks later, her grandmother picked us up from school and commented about how much time Laura had been spending in the pool because it looked like the sun was naturally highlighting her hair. We giggled in the backseat as we kept our secret safe.

I could always be myself with Laura. There were no fronts, no facades. It was just the two of us. In school, I didn't stick to a particular circle of friends. I was friendly with everyone, but Laura, she was my person, my other half. When I got in trouble or she got in trouble, even if we were grounded, our parents still let us go to each other's homes. Laura loved to snack, but there was never any junk food or soda at her house. My mom would pick up snacks from the grocery store just for Laura so when she came over, she could binge on them. My mom always knew if Laura had been at our house when she came home from work and saw the kitchen trash can full of Publix deli meat wrappers, Twinkie wrappers, and empty Coke cans. As soon as Laura would come into my house, she would make a sandwich, and grab a Twinkie and a Coke, faithfully. I've never bought a Twinkie since the accident. Laura was part of our family, and my mom felt the same way. My mom knows all about friends being considered family. In fact, that's where I learned it.

My mom also has a best friend. She met Mari in middle school, when she lived in Puerto Rico. After high school graduation, my mom came to St. Petersburg to go to Eckerd College. Mari was just across the bay, at the University of South Florida (USF) in Tampa. They visited each other on the weekends when they could. As the years went by, they each got jobs and started their own families. As kids, Mari's son and I went to each other's birthday parties. At times, my mom and Mari lived in different parts of the country, so they saw each other less often, but their friendship never changed. Whenever I saw Mari and my mom, I knew that's how Laura and I were going to grow up. We were going to be just like them. When Laura decided she was going to go to Eckerd College, where my mom went, it solidified that for me. She was going down the same path my mom did. I would be her Mari.

While I was making college decisions, my parents were finalizing my little sister's adoption. My sister joined our family during my senior year in high school. I did not want to go away to school. I wanted to be home and I wanted to be a part of my sister's life, so I applied to the University of South Florida–St. Pete campus, so that I could live at home. I could be a part of my sister's life, but I could still drive to school. Laura's school was not far from mine, and she lived on campus, so I could go hang out with Laura in her dorm room any time. We even started working at the same restaurant. We were completely inseparable.

Friday nights were always unknown at the restaurant. Were we going to be busy all night? Would I be stuck there super late? Would it be a quick rush at dinnertime and then clear out? One particular Friday night, I was hoping for the latter because as a freshman in college, taking 16 credit hours and working multiple jobs, I was just ready to go home. I had been working too much and studying too late, and I felt like maybe I was coming down with a cold. What I really needed was some rest.

Imagine my excitement when my manager told me that I could go home a little bit earlier than everybody else. I left the restaurant without looking back and headed home to crawl into bed. Then Laura called. She was still at work but getting ready to get off. Her roommate wasn't going to be home that night and we would have her whole dorm room to ourselves. After hearing that, I didn't really care if I wasn't feeling well. When would this opportunity come up again? I grabbed a big duffel bag, threw a bunch of clothes inside, and picked her up, and we headed to her dorm.

Once we realized there wasn't anything going on around campus, we decided we were going to have a girls' night out and go dancing. Laura loved to dance. We turned up the music as loud as it would go in her dorm room. We started dancing around like fools and trying on 20 different outfits (but of course ended up wearing the first thing we put on). I even borrowed one of Laura's necklaces to wear that night. We sat on the bathroom counter with our feet in the sink putting on our makeup, doing our hair, and taking silly pictures of ourselves in the mirror as we got ready.

When it was time to go we hopped into my car. It didn't matter to us who drove. We sang the entire way there with our windows rolled down and our favorite burned CD blaring through the speakers.

When we got to the club there was a long line outside. I don't exactly enjoy crowds, so when I saw the line I was immediately discouraged. *Maybe this wasn't a good idea.* It wasn't long before our wait in line came to an end. A man in his late 20s walked up to us and introduced himself as the hospitality manager of the club. He started to flirt with us and say how pretty he thought we were. He escorted us past the line and invited us right into the club.

We walked past security and through the front doors. Laura said, "I love this song," and we went straight for the dance floor. It was as if the world had stopped. Nothing mattered while we were there. Mid-terms, essays, and the stress of college instantly melted away. It was just the two of us having a girls' night out.

Laura wasn't very good at hiding what she was thinking. She wore her emotions (and opinions) on her face. As we were dancing, an unusual look came across her face and I knew something was wrong. She was looking over my shoulder at something or someone. When I turned around, the same guy who let us into the club was standing over a ledge watching us dance. Laura looked unsettled by his presence as he waved us over toward the bar. We looked at each other in confusion, wondering why he was calling us over. *Are we in trouble? Is he going to kick us out? He just let us in!*

We made our way through the crowd to the end of the bar, where he was. Turned out, we weren't in trouble at all. He asked, "Are you girls

21?" Laura and I looked at each other, neither knowing how to respond. But before we could say anything, he said, "It doesn't matter." He told the bartender to make us each a drink. "Two vodka–Red Bulls for the ladies." We felt like we were so special. Out of everyone in the crowded club, the hospitality manager was not only ordering us drinks, but he flat out said it didn't matter if we were 21 or not. We felt like we were on top of the world.

Once those drinks landed in our hands he quickly changed his mind. He said he didn't like the cups in our hands. He said it would be better if we switched to shots. He shouted, "Two Washington apples for the ladies" to the bartender. Things quickly became unsettling after that. He was taking pictures with us, asking for our phone numbers, and talking about hanging out later. Laura and I ditched him and made our way back to the dance floor—back to the two of us enjoying our girls' night out.

Before we knew it, it was 3 a.m. The club was closed, the lights came on, and it was time for everybody to go. Laura and I bolted out of the club, giggling as we took off our heels and ran barefoot to the parking garage. We did not want to get roped into having another conversation with that weird guy.

We got in my car, turned up the music, and headed home. Through the parking garage, Ybor City traffic, downtown Tampa construction, and across the Howard Franklin Bridge, it should have taken approximately 40 minutes to get back to Laura's dorm.

We never once discussed another option for getting home. We never once said that I shouldn't be driving. We never considered what could happen. We felt fine. We felt like it had been an innocent and carefree night. We had a few drinks and nothing was going to happen.

Five minutes from Laura's dorm something did happen.

Waking Up...or Not

"What's your name? Where were you going? What happened tonight?"

First responders were at my side, what was left of the car door between us. One of them continued to ask me questions. I kept interrupting him: "You need to help her. You need to help this girl. I don't know who she is, but she needs your help more than I do."

At the time, I couldn't understand why all of the paramedics seemed to be at my window and not my passenger side. I could hear him relaying things to the others about a head injury. I tried to reach up and feel my head, but he wouldn't let me. He grabbed my hand and held onto it the whole time he was there.

It was roughly 4 a.m. and I wanted to go to sleep. He continued to ask me questions and to try to keep me awake. I kept asking him to call my parents and repeating my parents' phone number. I didn't have the answers to any of his questions. I couldn't remember where I had been, where I was going, or who I was with, but I did remember my parents' phone number. I just kept repeating it over and over.

He said that it was really important they get me out of the car as soon as possible, and the only way they were going to be able to do that was to cut off the roof. I was terrified. "You can't do that," I yelled. "My dad is going to kill me!"

"Your car is totaled. Your dad will be happy you made it out of here. It's a miracle you're even alive!"

Covered with a large blanket to protect me from the debris, and clutching his hand the whole time, I vividly remember the car shaking and the terrifyingly loud noise. There I was, helplessly trapped in this dark, tiny space.

The next thing I remember, they were putting me into the ambulance, and then the bright lights. In the trauma unit, everyone seemed to be in a rush, cutting off my bloody clothes and hooking me up to machines. I couldn't understand what was happening. *Why is there such a panic? What is the rush?* Looking down, I had two arms and two legs. Wasn't I going to be okay? The nurse tried to be gentle as she cleaned me up, but the glass on my skin felt like thousands of tiny razor blades dragging across my body.

Just as the nurses finished taking my vitals and stabilizing me, a police officer arrived with a paper he asked me to sign. My signature would allow him to draw my blood and test for alcohol. *Is this normal protocol? Is he just pressuring me because my parents are not here?* I didn't know how to respond or if this was even legal. I asked the nurse, "Do I sign this? Is he allowed to be here? What's going on? I thought I was at the hospital. Why are the police here?" She told me she couldn't advise me. I wasn't sure if my parents had been notified I was at the hospital and I had no idea when (or if) they would be arriving. I was on my own to deal with this. The officer explained that Florida statute mandates drivers in what he called "this type of accident" are required to submit a blood sample for alcohol testing and reasonable force would be used if necessary. My blood sample would be taken whether I signed the paper or not. I was 18 years old and never heard of anything like this. *What am I supposed to do?* I cooperated and I signed the papers.

I later learned that what he meant by "this type of accident" was one that involved serious bodily injury or death, and he didn't come out and say those words because I didn't yet know about Laura.

The police officer came back into the room and asked me about a purse he found in the car. He wanted to know who it belonged to. I asked him to describe it. He said that it was blue, maybe more of a teal, and it looked expensive, like maybe it was an alligator material. I started to freak out. "That's Laura's bag. Laura was in the car with me. We had gone out together. Where is she?!" I tried to sit up in my hospital bed and look around for Laura. *Where is she?* He quickly left the room. He said nothing else.

Finally, my mom arrived. The look on her face told me I was in a lot worse shape than I thought. She told me that I had a very large gash on my head. She could see part of my skull and my ear was hanging, barely attached to my face. They were prepping me for surgery. I didn't care about any of that. I just wanted to know where Laura was. My mom didn't know, either. This was her first time seeing me, and all she knew was that I had been in an accident. She didn't even know someone else was in the car with me. I kept asking the nurses where my friend was. I told them I had known her my whole life. I kept trying to sit up in the hospital bed, but everything hurt. I lifted my head to look around the room. I was the only one there. The nurse said that the ambulance only brought me and it was her job to take care of me. That's all she knew. She wouldn't look at me when she answered my questions. I knew something was wrong.

Just before surgery, the police officer returned. He was getting ready to explain the forcible blood draw paperwork he had me sign as he pulled my mom just a few feet away from my bedside. The only thing I heard him say was "because this was a fatality." Now I knew. He was talking about Laura. Laura was the fatality. I started screaming and crying uncontrollably. "No, no! Laura's dead! I killed her. I killed my best friend. Her parents are going to hate me. I killed her." I was screaming and pulling out my IVs in a panic when the medical team rushed in to hold me down and sedate me. With five little words out of that officer's mouth, my world shattered into a million pieces.

Medicated, but still awake, I lay there lifeless for four hours as the surgeon administered more than 400 stitches to close the gash on my head and reattach my ear. Due to my severe head injury, I needed to be awake during the surgery. I lay there silent, convinced this was just a bad dream I was going to wake up from.

How could this possibly be real? A few hours earlier, my biggest concern was writing a paper or studying for midterms. Now what was I supposed to do?

Message: *Now What?*

There will be moments when life comes out of nowhere and punches you in the gut. Sudden loss, abuse, job loss, betrayal, health struggles—the list could go on and on. Whether the damage was done to you or by you, these moments leave us wondering: now what?

Give yourself a moment to catch your breath. You don't need to have it all figured out immediately. You won't. But if you're anything like me, you'll try to fix it. That's what we do when something is broken, right? We fix it.

We can't fix this.

The life/person/identity you knew before is gone. There is no going back. There is nothing we can do to change what has been done. We can't put the pieces back together; no one can. From here, it's our call. Will we leave the shattered pieces on the floor? Or will we pick them up and create something new from the mess?

What Can I Do?

Define where you are *right now*, not where you've been or where you're going.

Give yourself the space to process without trying to control the situation.

Believe that there is a new beginning right around the corner. It may get harder before it gets easier. But you have no idea just how strong you are.

Responsibility and Acceptance Don't Always Come Hand in Hand

Don't tell me it happened for a reason.

Trauma Tango One

From the moment I heard the words "because this was a fatality," I claimed fault. The accident and Laura's death were no one's fault but mine. I never once doubted that. However, I didn't always know how to express that to the world around me.

I lay in a hospital bed for a week. I wasn't allowed to walk or move. I wore a neck brace and a sling on my arm, and my head was completely wrapped in bandages. Unable to get out of my own bed, I was in a state of shock, convinced none of this was real. This had to be a bad dream I was going to wake up from. I was in a room by myself at the end of a hallway. Because I was involved in a serious crime, the hospital placed me under an alias for my protection. My name was listed as "Trauma Tango One"; Jessica Rasdall no longer existed. If you called the hospital looking for Jessica, they couldn't tell you I was there.

The doctor explained that if everything went as planned, I would likely be released within a week. To me, that meant everything would go back to normal in a week. This bad dream would last for a week, and then I'd be able to go home and everything would be fine. I would return to classes and school, and things would just go back to normal. Right?

My father came to my hospital bedside and explained that he had met with my university. Due to the circumstances, they were able to withdraw me from all of my classes rather than failing me. Rather than being relieved, I was furious. "Why would anyone assume I wanted to withdraw? I can go back to class next week. I've worked so hard this semester and I don't want to take these classes over again!"

I didn't understand. No matter how hard I tried, I couldn't seem to grasp reality. Nothing about the situation was real to me yet. I didn't understand that nothing would ever be the same. As I lay there in the hospital bed, I would grab the phone without thinking and dial Laura's phone number, only to hear her voice on the answering machine and be hit with the reality that I would never see her or hear her voice live again. There was no one to blame for that, but me.

From the moment I heard those five words—"because this was a fatality"—I never considered anybody else could be to blame. I did this. I took the drink. I put the key in the car ignition. I drove us home. Ultimately, the blood is on my hands.

Not everyone around me saw it the same way. People had good intentions and although they were trying to comfort me, every time I heard someone say that "Everything happens for a reason," I crumbled. I didn't believe that and it was the last thing I wanted to hear. Laura deserved to be here more than I ever did, and there was nothing fair about what happened. *There's no way this could have been for a reason. Why am I here and she isn't?*

Shock and grief have a funny way of warping reality. We all deal with things differently. We all process them in our own way and on our own terms. Nothing ever prepared me to take on the level of grief and guilt I did the night of the accident. Why is it that we have to pretend like everything's okay? Why do I do that? Growing up, I always wanted everyone to be happy—whatever that meant, whatever that looked like. I was the girl who laughed when she was uncomfortable and who was always smiling no matter what was going on. The one who was more concerned about making sure other people weren't uncomfortable, rather than showing how she truly felt.

Even though I was hidden in a hospital under a code name, friends from school somehow continued to visit. I hated every moment of that. As much as I appreciated everyone who came to check on me and show their support, I didn't know what to say. How are you supposed to face the friends you shared with the girl you killed?

Every time a visitor came to the hospital, I didn't know what to expect. What had they been told, how much did the story change, and what was their reaction to it? It's like playing the telephone game as a kid: With every person who tells it next, the story changes a little. How many people had told this story to someone else? How much of the truth did they actually know?

Each time the door to my hospital room opened, I was terrified about who would walk in next and what they would say.

Every flower, balloon, card, and visit—I didn't want any of them. I didn't deserve them. Who was I to have a hospital room filled with love when Laura would never make it to a hospital room? As our school friends came in to see me, though, I put on a smile. I made jokes. I pretended like everything was okay. The intense level of medication I was on made that a little bit easier, but I was existing in a weird, warped sense of reality. I would wake up in the middle of the night crying with nightmares and flashbacks alongside excruciating pain. The girl everyone knew was gone. Jessica was gone. There was nothing pretty about what was left behind of her. But I didn't want anyone to see that. I didn't want anybody to feel bad for me or feel sorry for me. I didn't deserve that. This was my fault and my fault alone.

Even though most of my hospital visitors arrived with a reaction of "That could have been me," not everyone felt that way. One relative exclaimed, "What were you thinking?" reprimanding me as I lay there lifeless, praying I would wake up from the bad dream. A few friends asked, "Why didn't you let her drive home? Why did you make her get in your car with you?" as if I had strong-armed Laura. In their minds, I set out that Friday night to achieve this result: I had planned to take a life.

After a week in the hospital, on March 2nd, I was finally released to recover at home. March 2nd was my 19th birthday. It was also the day of Laura's funeral. My birthday will always remind me of the day they buried my best friend. As the nurses helped move me from my hospital bed to a wheelchair, all of our friends started to show up. They had come straight from Laura's funeral to my hospital room. How are you supposed to process something like that? I can't imagine what they were going through. The mixed emotions they had been consumed with. How could they even look at me? Every time they said, "It was just an accident. This could have happened to anyone. Everything happens for a reason," it took everything in me to say thank you rather than lash out and respond with "No. This was my fault! I could've prevented it. I could've stopped this."

Searching for Answers

While I was recovering at the hospital, my parents were getting referrals for attorneys and researching who would be the best fit for my case. At that point, I didn't know I was being charged with a crime. I was clueless as to what would happen next. My parents kept the legal details hidden from me as I focused solely on my physical recovery.

Two weeks after the accident, I walked into my attorney's office with my parents for the first time. I didn't know what to expect, as I had never needed a lawyer before. Tim made me somewhat comfortable in the most uncomfortable situation. I felt like he had my best interests at heart and would do whatever he could to make the best of this horrible situation. I trusted him. I trusted him with my life and future. He informed me of the charges the state planned to file against me. Although we discussed how things would look going forward and what his plan of attack was, he made it very clear that I needed to understand one thing: No matter what we did during this case, I was to always remember I was facing 10 1/2 to 15 years in prison. That was the minimum guideline sentence for DUI manslaughter. That was my reality.

It was a big number to swallow. I had just turned 19 years old. Fifteen years in prison was almost as long as I had been alive. Tim would continue to remind me about that 15 years hanging over my head for the next two years. Every time we made some progress with the case or felt like things were going well, Tim was always that level-headed reminder:

"Even with all of the good work you are doing, please remember you are facing 10 1/2 to 15 years in prison. We can't forget that."

How did everything go so wrong in a split second? A split second that I couldn't even recall. No time in prison was going to bring Laura back. No time in prison would undo the pain, damage, and destruction I had caused with one choice. No time away would change any of that, though it still didn't sound like enough. In the coming weeks I kept looking for answers. *Why am I here and she isn't? How dare I survive when she didn't?* Putting her autopsy report and my trauma room report side-by-side, our injuries were almost identical, just on opposite sides of our bodies. The fact that I was a few inches shorter than Laura was the only thing that saved my life. What happened that caused this crash?

The initial accident report stated my car was traveling down the center lane of the highway. It spun off the road and rolled down the bank of the interstate. My car came to a stop when it rolled into a tree and bounced back to the ground. The tree crushed the roof of my car. There was minimal damage to the front and back. If you picture an empty soda can on its side, then someone stepping on it, the result is what my car resembled.

How did I make it out of that car alive? Why me? I felt like I had been left behind.

I found myself staying up at night reviewing my cell phone records, trying to decipher what happened the night of the crash. I called the last number on the phone history, the last person we talked with just moments before the crash. "Do you know what happened? How did we sound? What were we doing? Were we happy? Were we awake? Did I fall asleep? Did we suddenly hang up?" I needed an answer but I didn't know where to find it. Looking back, I can't imagine how that friend felt when I went to him for answers. I can't imagine how he felt knowing that, aside from me, he was the last person who talked to Laura that night.

I dug through the medical records and endless pages of hospital documents, reading and dissecting every piece of paper. The answer had to be hidden in there somewhere, didn't it? I wanted to know every detail, every conclusion, and every possible explanation for what happened. I was desperate for an answer. I needed to know why, though there was no answer.

As my attorney, my parents, and I tried to turn over every stone and figure out any possible reason for what happened that night, we needed to talk to the guy at the club who gave Laura and me the drinks. It's easy for people to quickly ask, "Well, what about the guy from the club? Isn't he at fault? He knowingly served you drinks when you were underage." That was much more complicated than people realize. The underage drinking incident happened in Hillsborough County and the accident happened in Pinellas County. There seems to be an invisible brick wall between the two, and trying to make a difference on either side is nearly impossible.

My attorney advised that we hire a private investigator to interview the man from the club. The investigator showed him the pictures of Laura and me with him. The investigation report stated: *"[He] advised that his job is to walk around the nightclub, making sure everyone is happy, are receiving their drinks and having a good time. He does not check ID's, he does not serve alcoholic beverages, he is more of a hospitality host. One part of his job is to move the prettier young ladies up to the front of the line and get them inside the club. He advised that he sees a lot of women and customers each night he works and these two females are not someone that sticks out in his mind or that he knows by name."*

A life had been lost and it seemed as though this man didn't even care. But it wasn't his fault. Even though his actions seemed wrong, the blood was not on his hands. He didn't force me to take that drink, and he didn't drive my car home.

I made those choices.

Responsibility and acceptance are not the same thing, and they don't necessarily go hand in hand. Even though I had taken full responsibility for what happened that night, I still hadn't accepted it. I was looking for every answer, for something to change it, for something to be different.

We All Deal with Loss Differently

We all want to be a part of something bigger than ourselves, but it's weird how that can impact us when trauma is involved. People want to be connected to it; even if it's something difficult or painful, they want to be involved and included. I never could have foreseen how that would impact my friendships during this time. When I was in the hospital and the accident ("Drunk Driver Kills Eckerd College Student") was all over the news, everyone came to visit. But some of those visitors were there to see other friends, because it had been on the news and they wanted to see for themselves. It was as though they wanted some piece of inside information, or they just wanted to say they were connected to this.

Once I came home from the hospital, charges were filed and reality set in. I was facing the emotional side of dealing with what I had done, and that's when everyone quietly disappeared. Most friends faded away, and I don't blame them. I couldn't imagine being in the middle of something like this, feeling like you would have to choose between supporting me or Laura. I would want to run from it. And that's what the majority of my friends did. They quietly disappeared.

A handful of friends stuck by me through it all. Some visited when I was in really rough shape, and others continued to let me know they were thinking about me, even when they didn't know what to say.

On the other hand, there were a few people who went out of their way to let me know that they did not support me. One in particular asked if she could come over to talk. I'm not sure why, but I said yes. I welcomed her into my home, into my bedroom—the four walls that were keeping me safe yet holding me hostage at the same time. This was my safe space and I allowed her to tarnish it.

We sat on the floor in my room and it was clear she'd come for one reason: She needed closure. She had some questions about her relationship with Laura that she wanted to ask me. She needed that final moment of peace. I gave it to her. I said everything she wanted to hear. Once she got what she wanted, she instantly transformed into a different person—a person I didn't know.

She was no longer there to see how I was doing or to mourn Laura's loss. It was no longer about Laura at all. The anger took over and she asked, "Why didn't you let Laura drive home? Why did you make her get in your car? Why did you do this to her?" She was convinced I intended for this outcome, as though I wanted this to happen. She made it very clear that she wanted me to go to prison and that I needed to "pay" for what I had done.

I'm not sure just how many times the story had been retold before it reached her. I have no idea what, or who, convinced her to come to my house, but I had never seen anything like this. In just a matter of seconds, it was as though I was sitting on the floor with two different people.

She wasn't the only one, of course. Other former friends reached out to express their anger. Some even wrote letters to the judge of my case in favor of a hefty prison sentence for me. I couldn't wrap my head around this. *Why are they interjecting themselves into my legal case if they were not with us that night?*

Maybe I was just too close to the situation to understand. I asked my parents, "What if it had been me instead of Laura? What if I died that night and Laura survived? Would you hate her? Would you want her to go to prison?"

Laura was a part of our family, and things weren't the same without her. My little sister reminded me of it more than I wanted. Catalina would come into my room, see pictures of Laura on my bookshelf, and ask me, "Why doesn't Laura come over to play with me anymore? Does she not like me?" I would just shatter into a million pieces. How could I look at this little six-year-old and explain to her what I had done—that she would never see Laura again? It wasn't her fault; it was mine. My sister had only been with our family for about a year at that point, had already lost one family, and was terrified of death. She was always worried about whether this new family would be permanent. What if we would be taken away from her like she'd been taken from homes before?

I wanted to do everything in my power to reassure her that we were her family—that this was her permanent home and nothing would change that—but how was I going to tell this six-year-old little girl, who was terrified of death, that her friend Laura wouldn't be coming over to play anymore, and that it was my fault? I couldn't. I hid it from her, in an effort to try to somehow protect her, but I think deep down she knew something was wrong.

What if it had been me instead of Laura? I continued to ask. I needed to understand. What if Laura drove and I was the one who died that night? How would my family feel about Laura? Would they hate her? Would they want her to go to prison? Neither one of my parents had ever experienced the loss of a child, or anything even close to it. My mom said that she could never put herself in Laura's mom's shoes and try to understand what she may be going through, but that, no matter how hard, she would have to respect the bond that Laura and I shared. Laura was considered family in our house, and my mom would have had a very difficult time wishing anything for Laura except for her to honor her friend's memory by continuing on with her life and achieving all the successes that she so well deserved and that were taken away from her way too early in her life.

Message: The Blame Game

In the first few weeks after the accident, the only thing keeping me going was the tiny little piece I had control over, and that's where the blame lay: in myself. Taking responsibility for my actions rather than pointing the finger somewhere else kept me somewhat in control. Controlling where I pointed the blame and the anger and the frustration—at myself—was a huge weight to carry.

Taking responsibility for my actions did not mean I had fully accepted what happened.

This is where the questions start to creep in. If you're asking yourself, *Why me? What if I had done something different? What's next? What am I going to do? Why did this have to happen? Why her/him? What if...?* please know that you are not alone. This is the first part of an ever-changing journey. We don't want to linger here too long. The "what if...?" questions will quickly become crippling. But don't worry. Together, we're going to shift from "what if...?" to "what is."

Before we can do that, though, we have to take responsibility for what we can.

Consider This

What are the pieces of _____ you can begin to take ownership of?

Where/for what are you currently placing blame in others or pointing fingers?

How can you begin to take responsibility for your own actions?

What pieces of the puzzle are you paying too much attention to in an effort to avoid your own responsibility?

Moving from "What if...?" to "What Is"

*And then you realize that you are
the author of this story.*

Therapy: What it Is and What it Isn't

I didn't start seeing a therapist immediately after the accident. I wasn't ready. I was in such a state of shock at that point and I wasn't ready to talk about it. I was distracted with physical therapy three days a week and countless doctors' appointments. But really, I was just too medicated to process anything more than making it through each day. A few weeks after coming home from the hospital, I started weaning off of the pain medicine and reality started to sink in. It hit me like a ton of bricks. I would force myself to stay up all night so that I wouldn't have to face those nightmares and flashbacks, and the reality that taunted me every time I closed my eyes. I would repetitively tell my family about that night, trying to process it. I kept asking them questions, hoping it would shed light on the answers I was desperately seeking. I couldn't keep doing that to them. I needed to talk to someone else. Three weeks after coming home, I knew it was finally time for me to see a therapist, but—full transparency—taking the leap to go to therapy was for a semi-selfish reason: I was hoping therapy would uncover an alternative truth to the one I was struggling with. As crazy as it may sound, I wanted her to uncover the pieces that I had blocked out—the pieces my brain wouldn't let me remember. Somehow I was convinced she would be able to get this out of me and I would find out exactly why this happened. I wanted therapy to be a fix-all.

That's not what happened. It was crippling to hear that in all my therapist's years of experience, she had never taken on a client with the level of survivor's guilt that consumed me. Just being alive was crushing me every single day. The weight of breathing was more than I could bear. I wasn't making the progress that I was hoping for in therapy. Then, during one of our weekly sessions, my therapist told me something that changed everything. She was very honest with me and told me that she almost didn't take me on as a client. She didn't know if she would be able to handle it. She told me a story of how survivor's guilt had crippled her own life and how she saw a lot of herself in me.

When she was a young girl, her older brother was looking after her. Her parents warned them not to go out on the frozen lake, but, as children do, they went anyway. The ice cracked and she fell in. Her older brother lost his life saving hers that day. She became consumed with the guilt of surviving when her brother didn't. But she didn't deal with that guilt for years. As most survivors do, she suppressed her feelings, as not to draw attention to herself. Years later she found herself immersed in work that would prevent others from being in the same situation. She started teaching children's swim lessons.

That shook something in me. That was the missing piece. That was going to be the answer: I needed to do something to prevent others from making the same mistake I had. That's the only way I could make a difference. That's the only way I would be able to find purpose in this pain.

Realizing what my therapist had overcome and seeing how she was changing people's lives every day by supporting them through the hardest times gave me a glimmer of hope in the darkness I felt lost in. She showed me her bucket list of things she was going to achieve in her life, and she had already crossed off quite a few big items: publish a book, raise a family, run a marathon. She was doing the things her brother couldn't do. Having a list of goals and achievements, and maintaining the motivation to pursue them, is incredibly hard when suffering from survivor's guilt. When your self-worth is in question it's a lot easier to give up on yourself than it is to give up on someone else. She taught me that going after those "bucket list" items wasn't about her at all. This resonated with me and changed my perspective on how to continue with my life and pursue my own goals and objectives.

Growing up, I learned that when I made a mistake, I addressed it and did my best not to repeat it. Though this was a mistake I certainly was never going to repeat, it was one I couldn't fix. I needed to prevent someone else from repeating my mistake. I refused to sit back and allow Laura to be forgotten—just another underage drinking statistic.

Stage Fright: Sharing My Story

Prom was coming up at the high school from which I had graduated. Every year before prom all the students gathered for an assembly. The principal would talk about the things we were allowed to do, what not to do, the dress code, and behavioral expectations. None of the students paid much attention. What if we did something different this year? What if maybe, just maybe, we could shake these students to the core? What if we set out to leave a lasting impact rather than just continue to go through the motions? I had just graduated the year before. I reached out to the principal and asked if I could come to talk to the students before prom. If I could let them see what was really going on behind the scenes and the new reality I was facing, maybe they wouldn't repeat my mistake. Maybe I could convince them to ask for help, make a phone call, or create a plan before being tempted with getting behind the wheel after drinking.

I was given the green light to speak. The thought of stepping onto that stage for the first time was horrifying. *How am I going to get on stage and relive the night of the accident?* Telling teens, "Don't do that!" doesn't work. It was time for something more impactful. What if we showed them the reality of the consequences of their decisions? What if the message came from someone who looked just like them, was their peer, and they could easily relate to? When I sat down at the computer and started writing my story, something incredible happened. I was forced to tell the story! I was no longer asking what happened and why it happened. Rather, I was telling others what I had been through. This changed everything. I was now the author of the story—not just a character. But this wasn't enough to prepare for actually delivering this content.

When I walked into that auditorium, I didn't know how I was going to get through the presentation. Not even a year earlier I was sitting in those same seats: I was a senior getting ready for prom. A year later I was getting ready to speak the most difficult words I would ever say.

Who am I to do this? How am I going to do this? It didn't help that my parents, Laura's and my mutual friends, former teachers, and a highway patrol officer were all in the audience. How are you supposed to openly share the biggest mistake you have ever made in front of all of them?

I wasn't necessarily ready to charge the stage and deliver a well-composed presentation, but I knew I was ready to make a difference. I got up there and read my presentation, word for word, off a piece of paper. I spent weeks writing this talk, but even with all the preparation I couldn't help but cry through most of my presentation.

I tried so hard to detach myself from the story I was telling; I tried to convince myself that these were just words on paper. I was going to read them and this would change the students' lives, but as I got to certain parts of the presentation, I could see the difficult words coming up out of the corner of my eye. I could feel my throat tighten up and tears fill my eyes as I anticipated what I was about to have to say.

There was nothing pretty about that presentation, but I don't think it could've been any more powerful than it was. I stood before an auditorium of teenagers, my peers, former teachers, friends, and family, and I confessed: "I drank, drove, and killed my best friend."

That day, I drew a line in the sand and decided to stop asking what my story was and start telling it. We found out the next week that nothing happened that year after prom. No students got in trouble. No one was arrested. There were no accidents. Maybe, just maybe, a life had been saved.

Days later, my dad received a phone call from someone who worked with him. I didn't know it, but his daughter was in the audience that day. He told my dad that he and his daughter had been fighting for weeks about her after-prom plans. When she came home from the presentation that day, she said, "I'll be home right after prom. I'm not going out."

Shocked, he couldn't understand why. His daughter explained the presentation at school that day and how I had told her about my decision to drink and drive. He thanked my dad from the bottom of his heart for me getting up there and being willing to share my story, despite it being exceptionally difficult, because of the impact that I ultimately made.

That wasn't the only phone call we got. Words of encouragement and affirmation via letters, cards, and calls started to flood in. I began to realize that maybe I could get through to these teens and show them my new reality. Maybe I could actually make an impact. I could keep Laura's memory alive and prevent her from being another underage drinking statistic. Maybe this is why I made it out of the car that night. It lit a fire in me, and I started speaking everywhere people would have me: high schools, colleges, youth groups, community groups, substance abuse facilities, churches. You name it, I was there. I took all of the money I had been saving up to move out of my parents' house and used it to fund these speaking opportunities. If these presentations could prevent another life from being lost, every penny I spent was worth it. But if I was going to go "all in" on this mission, I needed help. I couldn't do it alone, and I wasn't sure where to start.

Light at the End of the Tunnel

I started researching other stories of people who had taken their painful experiences and shared them with the world, and I was completely overwhelmed by the strength other people had to keep going. It was then that I found Bruce, whose story happened right in my own hometown, though I had never heard before. Bruce's wife and daughter were killed in an accident by a teen who was street racing. No drugs or alcohol were involved, just careless driving. The worst part of the story, though, was that Bruce happened to drive up on the accident scene. He witnessed firsthand his wife and daughter being burned to death in their car.

Now, one would think that an experience like this would leave him angry and vengeful, and it did at first, but when Bruce met the young man who took the life of his wife and daughter, he saw that the young man was going through something, too–that he was going to be left to carry this guilt–and Bruce wanted to do something about it. The offender, Justin, and Bruce set out on a mission. Bruce asked the judge to be lenient with Justin, to grant him a sentence that would allow him to tell his story, and the two of them shared the stage together, telling both sides of this tragic story. One, the man who lost his wife and daughter to a careless teen, and two, the teen who took those lives. It is an unbelievably powerful story, one that was told all across the country. Hallmark even made a movie about their story.

I needed to meet Bruce. I needed to ask him countless questions. He is someone who had clearly come out the other side of something like what I was experiencing. He knew way more about this than I did. I wanted to know where I should be speaking, how I could get involved with the work that he was doing, how I could support him and help him. This was the path. This would be a good first step. I reached out to Bruce, and he talked to me willingly. He made it very clear from the beginning that before I could ever speak at his events or I could ever volunteer, before we could ever move forward, he needed to know about me. He needed to know about my intentions—that this wasn't just some quick shot to try to get out of prison. He learned very quickly that it wasn't.

I started speaking with Bruce and volunteering at his events for teens around driving safety. He kept putting me in contact with more people who could help me get this message out to other community groups and organizations. He also introduced me to John. John was a young man who made a decision very similar to mine. When I told Bruce that I didn't know what to do from here, how to feel, what to think, what next steps to take—that I felt like nobody understood what I was going through—he pointed me in John's direction.

John's accident also happened coming home from Ybor City, Florida. It also happened on Interstate 275, and he was also a student at USF. The parallels in our story shook me to the core. It didn't even sound real. I couldn't believe it. Soon I found out that John's dad and my dad went to high school together, where they both ran track. What were the odds? This was no coincidence. Our paths were supposed to cross. Because, see, in those days, as much as I wanted to do this good work and as much as I wanted to keep going, there was always a voice in the back of my mind saying that if I didn't know what steps were next, if I didn't see anything in the future, if I couldn't envision what was coming, maybe this was the end of the road for me.

If I couldn't imagine how I would make it out the other side of this, maybe I wouldn't. John was placed in my life to be that light at the end of the tunnel. He gave me hope that I could make it through and that I could make a huge impact. When I first met John, he had already completed his prison sentence and come home to start his own life. He was still sharing his message, but he had gotten a job. He and his family were building an addiction recovery center on the beach. This situation, this mistake, this failure—it hadn't ruined his life. It had only put him on a different path, a path that would save more lives than he could ever, ever understand.

But, there was one thing very different between John's story and mine: The family of John's victim forgave him. They knew one young life had already been lost and they did not want to ruin another. A part of me always envied John and wondered why I couldn't have that. Bruce and John had stories of powerful forgiveness—forgiveness that I could never understand.

They weren't the only ones. They introduced me to more people just like them, like Renee, whose daughter and best friend were killed in a crash just like mine. Renee partnered with the driver responsible for their deaths to raise awareness about drinking and driving. She towed a trailer to each event. On that trailer was a chilling representation of the reality of drinking and driving: the crushed car that her daughter died in.

Looking back over the years, these powerful stories of forgiveness were placed in my life again and again. Every time I encountered one, it triggered tons of different emotions. First was an instantly overwhelming feeling of "Wow. What kind of person do you have to be in order to forgive something so horrible?"

They also made me question myself. If I were in those shoes, would I be able to forgive like that? Would I be able to put my own emotions aside and consider somebody else's? Meeting people like this also made me envious, because I wanted nothing more than to have that sort of forgiveness in my situation. It also made me hopeful. It was a reminder—a constant reminder—that sometimes when we go through the hardest things and we're hurt and we're broken, we can't always look somebody in the face and say, "I forgive you." Sometimes that happens quietly behind the scenes.

Bruce became my mentor and John was my "light at the end of the tunnel." I didn't realize how important it would be to have people like them in my life. I wanted to shut out the world and hide under my covers. But people like Bruce and John, they keep you anchored and focused on the good ahead. We can be so buried in the dark that we can't see a glimpse of the light. Allowing others to be the light for us can push us to achieve things we never knew were possible.

The New "What If...?"

A year and a half after the accident I was finally getting over the "what if...?" paralysis. I had accepted what happened, what I had done, and that I could never do anything to change it. And then an envelope arrived at my house. It contained a copy of the accident reconstruction report.

The report covered an examination of the mechanics of my car, the damage to the vehicle, and the accident site. It all seemed pretty straightforward until I reached the final paragraph:

"Since there was no mechanical explanation for the vehicle suddenly veering violently to the right, it must be concluded that there was input to the steering by the driver or occupant. I cannot speculate upon the reason for this sudden steering input, but it is not consistent with going to sleep and drifting off the edge of the road. It is not consistent with inattention."

I felt paralyzed with emotions. For the previous year and a half I had accepted the fact that my drinking led me to crash the car. Was this report suggesting something else may have happened on the road that night? Was it my inexperience as a young driver that ultimately caused the crash?

I continued to flip through the pages of report to find detailed photographs of the mangled metal that was left of my car. The Honda Civic resembled an empty can of soda on its side that had been stepped on. The front and back of my car looked untouched while the roof was completed caved in and the sides disfigured from the impact.

The photos captured my car from all angles: the tires, brakes, suspension, etc. However, there were two close-ups of an "abrasion mark" on my rear driver's side bumper. My car was now unrecognizable, so why would a little scrape be important? The description under the photos said *"abrasion marks showing striations consistent with contacting a concrete surface."* That instantly struck as odd. The accident did not involve any damage or impact to the front or back of my car. How did an abrasion mark get on the top of my driver's side bumper? There were no barriers or medians along the highway. Where did this come from?

My parents and I went to my attorney's office to learn more about the debriefing he had with the accident reconstruction specialist. He explained that the location of the abrasion, paired with the position of my steering wheel, implied that I may have over-corrected as a result of a hit to the back of my car. Someone might have hit me? He went on to explain that it looked as though another car tapped my back bumper, which resulted in an over-correction on my part. I locked my steering wheel to the right and spun my car off the road.

Instantly all of those "what ifs?" that I had pushed aside came flooding back. *What if someone else really did hit me? What if this wasn't a "cut and dry" DUI crash? Was there someone else involved in the accident? What happened? Why did I over-correct? If there was someone else, do they remember anything? Do they know what happened? Would they come forward? Do they know about Laura?* The "what ifs?" began to eat me alive again.

My parents reminded me of the reality that hit-and-run accidents happen every day. To add insult to injury, there were no cameras on that stretch of the highway, and no witnesses had come forward. The 911 callers reported the car on the side of the road, not the accident itself.

I had to keep telling my story. I needed to be the narrator. But this detail, I kept it to myself. I didn't want anyone to think I was trying to point fingers or shift the blame away from myself. This was my fault and my fault alone.

I poured into activities that would prevent others from repeating my mistake. I continued speaking and running the SADD (Students Against Destructive Decisions) chapter at the local high school. I pushed for legislation to keep bars 21 and up rather than 18 and up for females. I volunteered at DUI checkpoints. I dedicated my life to doing anything I could to stop another young life from being lost, but it was never going to be enough. None of these things would bring Laura back, and the more I did, the more criticism it brought.

Even with all of the speaking and therapy, it wasn't enough. I needed more help. My mental health was impacting my daily life. My therapist referred me to a psychiatrist, and he soon added three medications to my treatment plan: an antidepressant, an anti-anxiety medication, and a sleeping pill. Maybe taking these would help me function like everyone else. Maybe I would finally be able to get up in the morning and go to sleep at night.

But it didn't. I would fight the sleeping pills and stay awake late at night so that I wouldn't have to see the nightmares and replay the accident over and over again. It felt like there was no winning this battle within me.

Message: Rewriting the Story

I wanted someone to give me the answers—to fix this for me.

I spent so much time asking everyone around me, "What happened? Why wasn't it me instead of her? What if we had just called home?" These questions kept me in a state of denial rather than acceptance. It wasn't until I began to tell my story that I could begin accepting the truth. I took responsibility not just for my actions, but for my story. It became about the facts, not the questions.

Writing and speaking what happened that night (rather than asking someone else to tell me) forced me to accept my new reality. Acceptance was not something I intentionally sought. It was a byproduct of sharing my message. If I didn't know what was real and true, how would anyone else? Take control of your own story. It's time to start saying it, rather than asking for it to be told to you. The act of writing, telling, and accepting your story allows you to change the script from "what if…?" to "what is."

What Can I Do?

Stop asking and start telling. Even if you're not ready to share your story with the world, write it for yourself. Taking ownership of your story forces you to stop questioning and start narrating. By telling your story, you'll finally have a truth to being accepting. Write your story.

Identify people in your life who can be your "light at the end of the tunnel." Who has been down a similar path and made it out the other side? Use them as your anchors.

Gather and save all the positive feedback you receive. Save cards and letters. Screenshot and print any positive online feedback. Trust me: These will come in handy on the rainy days.

Rolling with the Punches

They'll try to stop you. Just keep going.

The Word Is Out and the Media Wants in

Remember how I said I've always been really concerned with keeping everybody else happy and doing whatever I can to keep the mood of the room light and airy? I just want people to live happy lives. I never wanted anybody to feel bad for me or pity me in any way. I don't do well with that uncomfortable feeling. That theme has been carried out through every presentation I've ever given. I have always struggled with receiving positive feedback. Survivor's guilt creeps in and cripples me. *I don't deserve that praise. I don't deserve to feel proud or happy. I'm just here to serve the audience and prevent another life from being lost.*

As good as it looked on the outside—that I was not giving up, pushing forward with my life, and speaking to tens of thousands of teens—a whole different war was going on behind the scenes. As hard as I was trying to keep Laura's memory alive and prevent someone else from repeating my mistake, someone or something would pop up and try to stop me. If one thing has remained constant on this journey, it's that you've got to be ready to roll with the punches. All of the speaking across the country drew a lot of attention. The outside world was convinced the only reason I was doing these things was to try to lighten my prison sentence. What the world didn't see was these actions and this activism were the only things keeping me going each day.

What I didn't expect would come from taking ownership of the story was the media attention. I couldn't understand why the media was so interested in my story. What was so special about me? Unfortunately, this type of story happens every single day. Why me? People found it unusual that I was not afraid to stand up and say, "I drank, drove, and killed my best friend" while there was a 15-year prison sentence sitting on the table. I was openly admitting my guilt across the country every time I said, "This was my fault. Please learn from me."

I never pointed fingers or wanted to blame anybody else. I knew what I had to do to prevent this from happening again. There's something powerful about that level of honesty and transparency, and the media wanted to share it with the world. I was terrified of that. It was only going to bring more criticism to me and to my family. Behind the scenes we were receiving harassing phone calls, emails, posts online, and even in-person threats. People were interjecting themselves into my legal case and making claims to my lawyer and judge that I was still going out and drinking, driving, and partying. The prosecutor claimed that I had no remorse and was "unaffected" by the tragedy that had taken place.

In reality, I was so depressed that I'd barely get out of my bed. My four bedroom walls held me captive as I battled the demons within. The guilt was eating me alive, and all I wanted to do was hide under my covers and wait for it to get better. But it wouldn't, and I couldn't. I knew I had a mission. I had to keep going. If not for myself, for Laura, who couldn't. How dare I stop when she never even had the chance to start? How dare I? How dare I even consider that? This is where the lesson I learned from my therapist came into play. It would have been much easier for me to give up on myself, but I was never going to give up on the legacy of Laura and doing everything I could to prevent others from having to face the reality that was haunting me.

In an effort to keep one foot in front of the other and distract myself while awaiting an inevitable prison sentence, I decided to take two classes at the university. *If I could just maintain some sense of "normal," I will be able to make it through this,* I thought. The first time we encountered the media I was in one of those classes. I had an exam that morning and then I was going to speak to a high school in the afternoon. My bag was buzzing; my phone was vibrating over and over and over again. It was my mom.

I stepped out into the hallway to call her back. "What's going on? I'm in class." She said, "Jessica, the news station is here at our home. They caught wind of your presentation this afternoon and they want to know if they can interview you, if they can attend your talk." I couldn't wrap my mind around this. One, how did they know about my talk; two, what were they doing at my house; and three, should I let them in?

I was so confused because half of me wanted to hide under a rock. I didn't want anyone outside of the student body where I was speaking to know about this. I didn't want to bring any additional attention to the destruction I had caused and the prison sentence I was facing. I didn't want anyone in my "normal life" to know the turmoil that was going on behind the scenes and in my head. It had been nearly two years since the accident, and I just wanted to quietly go about days until I would finally be sentenced. The other half of me knew that I was still here because I needed to make a difference. I was still on this earth because I needed to prevent other lives from being lost.

As much as I could go out and talk about this to schools, my impact would ultimately be limited to where I could speak. Allowing the media to come in and share my story in a bigger way would allow me to potentially impact more lives. I hesitated and I second-guessed myself, but I nervously said yes.

The media attention became more and more; it snowballed into something bigger than I could have ever imagined. I couldn't believe the day we got the phone call from ABC's *20/20* wanting to talk to me about a possible interview. Why on Earth would *20/20* be interested in talking to me? I was nobody. Nobody special. Unfortunately, this story happens every single day. Why me? I was so close to it that I just couldn't see that most people in my shoes were not taking ownership the way I was. They weren't sharing the experience.

To be honest, I didn't want to tell the story and share the experience. I didn't want to let anybody in behind the scenes. It already felt like I was getting criticism from every possible angle. Why on Earth would

I want to open the door for more harassment from strangers? The reality was, no external harassment could possibly compare to what was going on within me. I didn't want people to see the sleepless nights, the nightmares, and the medications I was on. I didn't want anyone to know how crippled I really was. I just wanted to keep putting on the happy face, showing up to these presentations, and serving my audience.

It was terrifying to get that vulnerable, so I said no. I said no to *20/20*, but the producers were persistent and kept coming back time and time again to explain the impact that I could have. To tell me about the difference that I would make. To assure me that this would be a project that I would be proud of. About a year later, I finally agreed to participate in the show. Agreeing to work with the media was nothing like I ever expected. They talk to you about the difference you're going to make and the impact you're going to have, but they never talk to you about the ugly side. They don't prepare you for how intrusive the interview process is. They are also very misleading, in that the story they portray to you in the beginning is not necessarily the story they publish in the end. They will say and do anything to make you feel good about the situation, but at the end of the day it's the network that decides the final product, not you.

The network flew my family and me to New York City to film the interview portion of the show. The host tried her hardest to get me to break down on camera. However, the heavy doses of antidepressants and anti-anxiety medication I was prescribed made that nearly impossible. I was a zombie. During a filming break she commented, "You're a tough young lady and much more difficult to interview than I expected." It felt like this was all a game to her. Her every move seemed to be a calculated tactic rather than a conversation. I wouldn't see the final product of the *20/20* special for another year. In the meantime, the reality of a pending prison sentence grew.

Back in the Courtroom

The prosecution hated that I agreed to share my side of the story with the media. The state prosecutor, Rohom Khonsari, was convinced it was an attempt to drum up pity and avoid my prison sentence. Over and over again he stated two points that I could never understand: one, that Laura and I had never been "that close" of friends; and two, that I had no remorse for my actions and all of my efforts were "a show."

How on Earth could he think that? Every time I looked in the mirror I saw a murderer. I saw a young woman I didn't recognize: someone who surely didn't deserve to be here more than Laura did. Every time I smiled or laughed, I felt guilty for a moment of joy when I had stolen that from countless others. When I looked at my little sister I was reminded that Laura's sister would grow up without her big sister. Every sleepless night tormented me with images of Laura in my passenger seat. Every scar on my body was a reminder of the damage that could never be undone. With every doctor's appointment, physical therapy session, and therapy visit, I felt guilty for surviving another day.

I understood why Laura's parents were upset, but what did I do to this man to make him hate me so much? Why had he made it his mission to crush what was left of me? I didn't understand his motives.

My attorney suggested I meet with a forensic psychiatrist to address the rumors that were flying around about my lack of remorse. It was time to get an outside opinion on my mental health and level of guilt. I didn't understand the point of this. I was already seeing both a psychologist and a psychiatrist more than I wanted to admit. Why did I need to see someone else?

I was instructed to pack a lunch, as I would be spending the entire day with the forensic psychiatrist. That was all I knew. I didn't know what else to expect. I assumed it would be just like another therapy session.

I had gotten used to that, considering I was going to therapy multiple times each week. When I arrived at the forensic psychiatrist's office, I was instructed to take multiple written tests. These were the type of tests that ask you the same questions over and over in different ways so you can't fake your responses. It felt like the questions would never end.

After a break for lunch, it was time for the interview.

The woman was so cold. She seemed emotionless as she asked me personal/intrusive questions for hours. She gave me no comfort with regard to my responses. She just listened and asked more questions. It was obvious she had interviewed some interesting characters throughout her career. She proudly displayed newspaper articles framed in her office of cases she had worked on involving serial killers and rapists. She had zero response to anything I said; it seemed like she had "heard it all" and I was just another seat in her chair.

When our time was up, she showed me to the door and that was it. No diagnosis, no comments—nothing. I left her office feeling exposed and vulnerable. This woman spent hours ripping me apart, tearing down every wall I built, and never took a moment to pick up the mess. What on Earth would her report say for the court? I couldn't imagine.

My attorney never shared with me the details of her report. I learned why he kept that from me at a court date two years after the accident. The forensic psychiatrist took the stand and began to deliver her analysis. Again, she seemed unaffected by anything she said. With an emotionless expression, she told the court that I had an extreme case of PTSD (post-traumatic stress disorder), survivor's guilt, depression, and anxiety. The prosecutor interrupted her: "Wouldn't you be upset if you killed someone? Wouldn't anyone be upset?"

She immediately got upset that he was questioning her work and replied, "No, that's not what I said. I didn't say she's upset." She hesitated with her next statement. She paused and looked back at me. For the first time, she looked at me with an expression: pity. I could tell she didn't want to say what she was thinking. She turned back around to the judge and prosecutor, and said, "That girl has the worst case of survivor's guilt that I have seen in my entire career. She will never be the same again."

Rohom muttered, "I have no more questions."

I felt violated—as though somehow everyone in the courtroom had seen a side of me that was supposed to stay private. What are you supposed to feel when someone says you'll never be the same? Are you supposed to give up? Is this where people throw in the towel? It shook me to the core, but I refused to let it define me. I may have the worst case of survivor's guilt she's ever seen, but I refused to allow that label to define me.

As the months went on, my psychiatrist continued to increase my medication dosage. It wasn't working like we had hoped. I was still extremely depressed and staying up all hours of the night. In the morning, I felt like a zombie and didn't want to get out of bed. I was just a shell of the person who used to be there. I was numb inside.

My medication arrived in the mail. (That's the way our insurance worked.) One month, my prescription was late. Not taking my medicine for a few days threw my body into severe withdrawals. I was dizzy and throwing up, and I had never felt like that before.

All I could think was, *What if I go to prison and they don't give me my medication?* I couldn't imagine being thrown into that new, unknown environment while feeling sick like that. That thought terrified me, and it was a wake-up call: It was time for me to get off of the medication for good. I needed to get off of the antidepressants and to finally feel all of the emotions I had been suppressing. If I didn't start feeling these emotions, I was never going to move through them. But more importantly, I was terrified of going to prison on medication.

I went to my psychiatrist and I asked him to take me off the pills. He refused, claiming, "It's too dangerous. You'll be a threat to yourself and others." I was so discouraged. *Why doesn't he believe I can do it? Why doesn't he think I am strong enough?* I knew I couldn't just stop taking the medication cold turkey; I needed help. I went to my primary care doctor and she helped me wean off of these medications in a slow, safe way over the course of three months.

But then everything was real. No more medication to mask the pain meant I felt, saw, and heard everything that seemed like a blur before. I wasn't sure how long I could bear feeling all of these emotions before I would break. Waking up every morning with the unknown sitting on my chest made it difficult to breathe. The legal side was out of my hands, and I needed it to come to an end soon. Until there was a sentencing, I wouldn't be able to accept that part of my story. I wasn't sure how much more uncertainty I could handle without medication, and I was ready for some closure.

Regardless of what the media portrayed, and no matter the picture the prosecution tried to paint, I knew that I was making an impact. I would never be able to measure the impact I had made. We would never know how many lives had been impacted. There was no way of knowing if, in fact, a life had been saved. I just had to have faith that I was making a difference, and the feedback from parents, students, and teachers was assuring me that I was.

I spoke to more than 15,000 young adults during the two years my case was open. That had to have a made a difference, right? At least one life had been saved along the way, hadn't it? But none of that mattered. I still had a legal case sitting on the table. Nothing was going to change the fact that I was facing 10 1/2 to 15 years in prison, and I might just have to give up making this impact for quite some time.

That was such a difficult thing to process. Part of me didn't think any kind of punishment would ever be enough, while another part of me didn't want to stop speaking for a second. What if there was another life I needed to touch? What if there was somebody else who needed to hear me? How was I ever going to prevent this from happening again if I couldn't continue to share my story? What good would a day, a year, or 15 years in prison do? Nothing was ever going to bring Laura back.

The only thing I wanted to do was prevent someone else from repeating our mistake. But none of that mattered. Through the ups and downs and emotional rollercoaster of this open case on the table, I'd finally reached my breaking point. As much as I wanted to keep sharing the message, raising awareness, and doing this prevention work, I needed to finally have some closure.

I drew a line in the sand and decided it was time to move forward. I had to do something to put this legal case behind me.

Preparing for Closure

The night before my final court date, I sat down with my little sister to explain what was going on. She had no idea about the legal ramifications. She didn't even know that Laura had been in my car that night. How was I supposed to explain to a little girl that her big sister was going to leave her? I sat her down and began to explain punishment in terms I thought she would best understand.

"Catalina, you know how when you make a mistake sometimes you are put in 'time-out' to think about what you did? When we're adults, the same thing happens, except that 'time-out' sometimes means we have to go away for a little bit. When you drive a car, you're responsible for everybody in the car. That's why Mom always tells you to put on your seat belt and to behave in the car. When we drive the car, we have to make sure everyone is safe. When I was in my car accident, I wasn't alone. There was someone else in my car."

She interrupted me and asked, "Was Laura with you? Was it Laura?" Trying to get the words out through the tears, I mumbled, "Yes, yes it was. And Laura didn't make it. She never made it out of the car that night." Catalina asked, "Is that why her parents are mad at you?" And I said, "Yes." And with the innocence of a child she just responded, "But it was an accident. Laura isn't mad at you." It's crazy how such a young kid could have such a clear perspective.

I explained to her that the next day I would be going to see the judge, and this time it might be the last appointment. I might be punished and not come home afterward. I didn't know what was going to happen. I didn't know if I would go away or for how long I would be gone. But I needed Catalina to know it wasn't because of her—that me leaving had nothing to do with her. I would be home eventually.

I tried to be tough for my sister, and I didn't want her to see how scared I really was. I had no idea what was going to happen the next day and what those following years would look like. We see the shows on TV. Our culture is obsessed with crime and punishment. There are more shows on TV about jail, prison, court, and crime than I can name. But watching those shows in no way prepares you for what you're about to experience. How are you supposed to mentally prepare for something when you have no idea what it's going to be like? I had never been in trouble before. I came from a good family and had more opportunities than I deserved. I didn't know the first thing about jail or prison. I was terrified. *Will I really make it through? How would it even be possible? Not me. I'm not going to be strong enough for this. How could I be?*

Deciding My Fate

I had been appearing at court dates every single month since the accident. On May 23, 2008, two years after my crash, I walked into the courtroom for the last time. It was supposed to be just another court date (a monthly check-in), but I had reached my limit. Two years of court dates, therapy, interrogations, doctors' appointments, advocacy, and harassment—I was done. I surrendered myself to the judge and begged him to sentence me. I arrived with a statement to read to the court and Laura's family, but I couldn't get through a single sentence of it. There I was, the girl who had given presentations all across the country to tens of thousands of people, but I couldn't even read a sentence out loud.

Every time I stepped into that courtroom I was crippled with emotions. My body would tremble, my palms would sweat, and my stomach would turn. I became physically ill the morning before every court date. Once it happened just outside the courthouse, just before walking in the doors. Even if it was just a court date to reschedule, walking into that building made all of those nightmares come to life.

All of those emotions that I held back in front of everybody else, I couldn't hide them there.

The second I opened my mouth to read my statement, I began shaking and crying hysterically. I thought I was ready. I guess not. I tried so hard to read my statement, and I couldn't. Finally, the judge asked my attorney, "Can you please assist her?" As he came to read my statement to the courtroom, my knees grew weak. All I was able to get out was, "I drank, I drove, and I killed my best friend. I'm sorry. I'm so sorry." My attorney finished the rest of the statement.

There was never a doubt in my mind that this was my fault. There was never a doubt in my mind that I was the reason Laura wasn't here. I asked the judge to sentence me with something that would allow me to continue sharing this message—something that would allow me to continue to do this work. My psychologist suggested house arrest, where I would be able to continue treatment and my outreach efforts.

By surrendering myself to the judge the way I did, anything was possible. The guideline sentencing for DUI manslaughter, the charge I was facing, was 10 1/2 to 15 years in prison, but the possibility of a youthful offender departure was still on the table. Essentially, in the state of Florida, if you are under 24 years old, and have never been in trouble before, you are considered a "youthful offender" and could have your maximum sentence reduced to six years, with no more than four of those spent in prison.

So the judge had to make a decision in an incredibly divided courtroom. One half of the room was asking for leniency so I could continue to raise awareness about drinking and driving. The other half of the room was asking for the maximum sentence. How was he supposed to make this call? For two years, this judge sat on this case. He listened to our heartbreaking stories, he watched us break down and cry, and he maintained a straight face when I couldn't speak before him.

I'll never understand the weight that he's carried from that. I'll never know how many sleepless nights he had and how much this decision taunted him, but I am so sorry that he ever had to be a part of this. When it came time to declare a sentence for this crime, the decision was solely in his hands.

After my attorney read my statement, the judge spoke. His words surprised me. Throughout this entire case he had seemed to be emotionless. While I know that came with the territory, I was surprised when he said, "Now Ms. Rasdall, I don't have to say any of this. I'm not required to, nor should I, but what you've done during this case is to be commended. You've worked very hard to impact young lives. It's something you should be proud of." I couldn't believe it. The judge, the man getting ready to sentence me to prison, was telling me he was proud of the work I had been doing. It broke my heart. I was letting down someone else— another life I had tarnished by my decision that night—but he had the courage to commend my efforts. I can't thank him enough for saying those words. It kept that fire burning in me to keep doing this work. If he of all people could see the impact I was making, surely I was making a difference in this world.

He explained to the courtroom how both sides of the case were feeling. He acknowledged everyone and said he would meet us in the middle. He offered me a youthful offender departure but it would have to be the maximum sentence. That meant I was offered four years in prison followed by two years of probation. This was a six-year split sentence, but I had to make a decision right away.

I asked for a moment to speak with my parents and my attorney. He told me to make it quick.

We were escorted to a door in the back of the courtroom. Seated in a windowless room, at a table with my parents and my attorney, I asked, "Okay, what do we now?" Everyone paused for a minute. They looked at each other in silence. They finally said they had supported me on this whole journey and would continue to support me. They said they would be by my side through this, but they couldn't make this decision for me. Ultimately, I was the one who had to serve the prison time and I alone had to make the call. I had to say yes or no to the plea deal. No one could do that for me.

I was instantly overwhelmed with emotions. I had an anxiety attack in the hallway of the courthouse and began to hyperventilate. I couldn't breathe. The weight of my decision, the weight of the pain I had caused, and the gravity of this decision crushed my chest like a thousand bricks.

I had two choices. I could say yes right then, in which case I would be immediately handcuffed, shackled, and taken to prison, where I would spend the next four years of my life. I would be a convicted felon, have my driver's license revoked and voting privileges taken away, and forever have to check the little box on job applications that makes employers toss it in the trash.

On the other hand, I could say no, and we would prepare for trial. If I went to trial, there would be one of two possible outcomes. If we went to trial, the prosecutor would have to prove to a jury that I was guilty beyond a reasonable doubt.

In the state of Florida, DUI manslaughter occurs when a person:
    (1) Drives a vehicle, or is found to be in actual physical control of a vehicle, within the state of Florida;
    (2) And the person is either:
        (a) Under the influence of alcoholic beverages or any chemical or controlled substance, when affected to the extent that the person's normal faculties are impaired; or
        (b) Has a breath-alcohol level of 0.08 or higher; or
        (c) Has a blood-alcohol level of 0.08 or higher.
    (3) And causes the death of another person, either directly or indirectly.

If the jury had any reasonable doubt as to what caused the accident resulting in Laura's death, they would have to pronounce me not guilty. I would walk away with nothing, not a scratch on my record. But if the jury found me guilty, I would spend 15 years in prison.

The possibility of walking away without a conviction was heavier than the reality of four years in prison. I couldn't stomach the idea of leaving that courtroom without some form of punishment. It sounds crazy to write this, as I knew no time in prison would change what I've done. No time in prison would bring Laura back. Prison doesn't heal wounds and nothing good results from it. But in my mind, Laura wasn't here and I was. It wasn't fair that only one of us made it out of the car that night. I needed this—the closure. I needed to be convicted of this charge. I needed to be convicted of her death.

I was ready to get away from everything, every place, and every person who reminded me of what I had done. It all reminded me of Laura. The four walls of my bedroom at home felt as though they were closing in on me. How much worse could a prison cell really be? I needed to feel as though I paid my price. I was ready to do that.

We walked back into the courtroom 20 minutes later. As soon as I signed my name on the bottom of the plea deal, a strange sense of calm came over me. I could breathe again. Although I was terrified of what was ahead, I knew I made the right decision. Within seconds of signing the paper, I was handcuffed, shackled, and taken to prison, where the next part of my journey would begin.

But this wasn't going to stop me from sharing my message.

Message: It's Not About Us

Just when you feel like you're finally making progress, you'll get thrown a curveball. Is it frustrating? Absolutely. Does it keep you on your toes? Certainly.

Adversity forces us to revisit our motivates and mission: Why are we doing this work? Who is it serving, and why?

If we're on a solely self-serving mission, adversity can cause us to throw in the towel. It's easy to give up on ourselves when things get hard. We're our own worst enemy, after all. We have to be motivated by something, or someone, bigger than just ourselves. We have to believe that our actions impact others.

Giving up on ourselves is much easier than disappointing someone we love.

In the most difficult of days I reminded myself, *Laura can't even begin this journey. How dare you even consider quitting?* I focused on the lives that could be impacted by this work. I believed that someone out there was alive today because of these presentations. Even when we can't see or measure our impact, we must have faith that it's there.

Don't allow adversity or criticism to stop the progress you've worked so hard to make. As for the individuals dishing it out? With time, some may come back around (maybe even the people you least expect). But we can't force it. The only thing we can do is remain consistent in our actions.

Consistency speak volumes. Keep doing the work you've been called to do. Your consistency will change hearts and minds.

What Can I Do?

Revisit the positive feedback you've been saving. When adversity creeps in, allow the words of others to keep you focused on the progress you've made.

Call on help. You don't have to do this alone. Establish an inner circle of family, friends, or mentors who can keep you grounded. When criticism rolls in, whom can you call to remind you of the good work you've been called to do?

Determine who (or what) is driving you. Who (or what) will carry you through the difficult days? Who is your inspiration and driving force behind the scenes? Who do you refuse to let down?

People can be cruel. We do things out of fear or anger that we don't necessarily understand or mean. It's time to start developing "rhino skin." Prepare yourself for those uncomfortable moments of confrontation behind the scenes in a place that feels safe to you. Ask yourself:
- What could they possibly say to me?
- How much of this is factual?
- How much of this is fabricated or spoken out of fear/hurt/anger?
- How can I respond in a way that acknowledges their feelings, but protects my own?

Practice, practice, practice. Get comfortable navigating difficult conversations.

- What questions or conversations are making you uncomfortable? Take note of those and practice responding to them with a trusted friend. When they do come up, you'll be ready to respond without feeling paralyzed in the moment.
- What are the questions you fear others will ask? List them all out on a piece of paper. Next to each question, prepare a response in private. Share your response with a trusted friend to see if any follow-up questions may arise.
- Practice saying, "I'd rather not talk about that right now." You don't have to please everyone. Define your boundaries and hold them close. Just because someone asks a question, doesn't mean you have to answer it. Get comfortable politely declining conversations that are too difficult to bear.

Labels: Own it or it Will Own You

Take ownership of your mistakes, but don't let your mistakes define you.

From College Campus to Correctional Institution

Signing the plea deal opened up a new world to me. I was no longer the girl in the accident waiting to go to prison. I was now inmate #154809. I was a convicted felon, a criminal, a convict. I would be reminded of those labels for the next four years of my life.

When you're booked into the system, you are strip-searched and sanitized, and have all of your belongings taken from you. Everything you knew and believed to be true, including the name you called yourself, is gone. The person before incarceration no longer exists. You are now a DC (Department of Corrections) number. You are a number and that's it. When I was issued the card, which I still have, I couldn't believe it. My identity was now this little piece of plastic. I was now inmate #154809. How did the girl I knew—the daughter, sister, friend, college student—become an inmate in state prison? Where did *she* go? What happened to her?

As I was booked into prison, I had to complete medical, psychological, and educational evaluations. When I arrived at the psychological evaluation, the woman told me they were going to put me on antidepressants. I refused.

I pleaded, "Ma'am, but I don't need medication. Please don't prescribe those." Very seriously she responded, "Yes, you do. With your charges and the amount of time you have here, there's no way you're going to be able to handle this. You won't be able to survive this without it."

I was so upset. How dare she tell me what I was capable of handling? She had no idea what I had been through over the previous two years. I tried to explain to her that I had already been on medication and successfully taken myself off. The last thing I wanted was to feel like a zombie again. Again she urged me that I had no idea of the road ahead and that I was going to need medication to make it through this. Again, I politely declined.

Angered by my refusal, she told me that if I refused to take medication, she would be forced to place me at the highest security level. I was considered a threat to myself and a threat to others on the prison compound. I would remain at a maximum-security facility until they felt I was no longer a threat. How dare they punish me for refusing antidepressants?

After evaluations, I began the walk to the dorm I would now call "home." A corrections officer escorted me there with another young girl. I didn't know her. I didn't know anything about her charges or why she was there. Each of us was carrying a small, clear, plastic trash bag that held all of our belongings: an extra state-issued blue inmate uniform, a set of white sheets with the elastic removed, and the toiletries I brought from my week in county jail. That was our property now. As we walked down the hill to the dormitory, I didn't even have to question which building it was. All I could hear were the girls screaming obscenities at us out the window. It was like something you'd see in a movie—except this was real and that building was about to be my home. I can't explain how heavy and hard my heart was beating. The unknown is always scary, but I was expecting and picturing the worst. We stood in front of the door, and they unlocked it and let us in. I jumped as the steel door slammed behind us. We were immediately taken into the officer's station, where they checked our belongings and assigned us to a bunk bed. I wasn't expecting a warm welcome, but what I received was something I'll never forget.

The officer in charge of the dorm was clearly ex-military. He was a very large man and was screaming in our faces, just like drill sergeants do in the movies. His job was to shock us in—to break us down. The youthful offender program was a military-based program. My first encounter with this program was being screamed at an inch from my face. The girl next to me was crying hysterically, but I just stood there. I didn't say a word. I deserved this. He asked her about her charges and she told him through the tears that she was there for violating probation. She had prior drug charges. He asked her if she had children and she said yes. He went on to degrade her, and tell her how bad a mother she was and that her children would end up just like her. I don't think I've ever heard the word "worthless" so many times in my life. Then he turned to me and asked why I was there. He asked, "What? Did you forget to return a library book?" I guess he didn't think I looked like I belonged here. *Why? Because I wear glasses?*

I looked him straight in the eye and said, "I drank, I drove, and I killed my best friend." He didn't really know how to respond to that. He paused for a minute and said, "You took a life. Somebody's family is destroyed over this. You know that, right?" I responded, "Absolutely. I think about it every single day and I see her every time I close my eyes."

When you have to explain to somebody why you're in prison and you say the words "DUI manslaughter," they don't get full the picture. They have no idea of the guilt and the grief that are silently eating you alive. They have no idea of the tens of thousands of teens you have spoken to, of the awareness you have tried to raise, that you had dedicated your life to making this right. They don't see any of that. All they see is another DC number. They see a felon who is going to commit the crime again.

He asked the other girl to leave the room. He got out of my face and he sat down in his chair. He began to speak to me like a human, not a dog. He asked me to tell him a little bit more about the story so he could understand.

When I owned up and told him why I was there, it was like he had never heard anybody say that. He told me, "There's a couple girls in here I'm going to need you to talk to. They're here on similar charges, but they're not taking it the same way you are." In that moment I realized that maybe, just maybe, in this place of complete darkness, anger, and hate, there was a possibility that I could be the light for someone else. I knew that I was going to impact some lives over those next four years, but I wasn't sure how.

The College Convict

When I was shown to my bunk, the girl in the bed next to me immediately spotted my hygiene products. Prior to being transported to the prison, I spent a week in county jail. My shampoo, conditioner, and deodorant from county jail were different than what was available in state prison. If you've been in prison for a while, anything new is exciting. She asked if she could buy them. I calmly looked over at her and said, "Look, I'm going to be here for a few years—I'm not just passing through—so I think I might need these. Sorry." She had this smirk on her face, but said, "I get that. Okay." (Keep in mind I didn't have a lock for my trunk at the time, and she could have easily taken anything she wanted, but she didn't.) She respected me taking ownership and saying, "Hey, I need this. I'm going to be here."

I sat on my metal trunk, which now contained everything I owned, and looked around the room at 74 young women staring back at me. It was an open dorm with metal bunk beds lining the walls. In the middle of the room were single beds to keep the sight lines open from the officer's station. In the front of the room was a large single standing fan. The women were arguing over which direction the fan would be pointed, as there was no air conditioning in the dorm. *Who are these women? How did they get here? Where did things go wrong for them?*

Who knew you could feel so alone in a room with other 74 women? Prior to my sentencing, I didn't realize just how badly I needed to be alone. Throughout the whole period between the accident and sentencing, I felt like I kept myself very isolated, and I stayed within those four bedroom walls at my parents' house more than I probably should have. But I was still living in the same town that I had when Laura was alive. I was still going to the same places we went together and passing restaurants where we ate together. Everything and everyone reminded me of her. Everything and everyone reminded me of the pain I had caused, the lives I had shattered, the damage I could never undo. There was something about being isolated behind this razor wire on this metal bunk bed that finally gave me a sense of relief.

It wasn't about Laura and me anymore. It was about my punishment. I didn't want the sentence to happen. I didn't want to stop doing the work I was doing. I didn't want to stop raising awareness. Every day behind those gates I felt like I was allowing this to continue to happen in the world—that I had somehow given up. But maybe I needed a break. Maybe I needed that time, that space, that separation from what Laura and I had together. Maybe that's just what I needed in order to finally find forgiveness.

Prior to going to prison, I had never looked at education as an opportunity; it was more of an obligation. I had to get up for school, show up, do the homework, write that paper, or study for that test. It was never that I *got* to do that. I had gone through school, I had started college, and I was not an outstanding student. I was average at best. I was an A or B (and an occasional C that would get me in a lot of trouble with my parents) student. I tested well but I hated doing homework.

When I got to prison, it blew my mind to meet these other young women, younger than I was, who had children and couldn't read books to their kids. How was this possible? Didn't these girls go to school like I did? How were these young women not getting an education? How would there ever be hope for them after prison? They were doomed to come back.

A few months after arriving at the prison, I started taking correspondence classes and continued college classes through the mail. When the prison education department caught wind of that, they offered me a job within the school at the prison. This meant that I would be able to work with the girls in my dorm and tutor them as they worked to earn a high school education. This was a serious advantage for me. I was going to be building a new level of trust with the women that I lived with, and I was going to be able to help them. That's the one thing that would keep me going. That's the thing, throughout this whole stage of the journey, that anchored me. Helping others was the only thing that gave meaning to me being alive.

These women gave me a new perspective on education, one in particular. She was my first one-on-one mentee. When I met her, she was pregnant. She was pregnant in prison, and she would have her child there. And then her child would be taken away from her. I couldn't imagine. When we first started working together, she was reading at a sixth-grade reading level. She was going to be released soon after the baby was due, so her sentence was ending, and I was going to do everything in my power to make sure she got her GED before she left.

We studied day and night. We took practice tests together. I even remember writing home to my parents, so proud that she passed. I felt that if I couldn't help her get her GED, I was condemning her to come back. How was she going to raise this child, who was born in prison, if she couldn't get a job? Helping these women earn their education gave them a second chance, and that gave me a purpose.

While I was cleaning the dorm one afternoon, an officer came in. He was working on a crossword puzzle and was stuck. I love puzzles. I always have. He couldn't figure out something and was getting really mad at himself. He mentioned it to the other officer. I overheard, and quietly, under my breath, muttered the answer, and it was right.

Shocked, he looked over at me. "And who are you, and why do you know that?"

The other officer responded, "She's the one who works in education. She's the one taking those college classes in the mail."

"So you're a college convict, huh?" He was making a joke of it, not being mean or cruel. That's just the way he was. He had me finish the puzzle for him.

A few days later, at count time (when everyone has to sit on their bunk while the entire prison population is counted to account for every inmate; no one is allowed to move or talk during count time), all of a sudden, that officer came barging into our dorm over the intercom. "College convict, come to the officer's station."

I walked up there, thinking that I was in trouble. Instead he had another puzzle that he couldn't solve. He wanted my help. He'd come all the way across the compound to have me help him finish a puzzle. For the student who always felt less than average, this was quite a boost to my self-esteem.

Even though he thought this was funny, and he was very nice about it, not everybody was like him. I remember one day going to visitation to see my parents, who were visiting me. That same officer was standing at the top of the hill with two other guards. As a youthful offender, you're not allowed to walk around the prison compound by yourself. You have to be escorted, and in order to pass another officer, you must stand at parade rest (feet 12 inches apart, legs straight without locking the knees, hands at the small of the back with fingers extended and thumbs interlocking, and your head and eyes forward) and ask, "Permission to carry on, sir." They determine if you can go or not.

I knew one of the guards at the top of the hill was a real jerk (I'll call him Officer Smith), so I wasn't looking forward to getting up there. As I stood at parade rest and asked for permission to carry on, he just looked me up and down.

The other officer said, "Good morning, college convict."

Officer Smith was noticeably confused. He said, "College convict? Why are your teeth so white?"

I didn't really know how to answer. "I don't know, sir. I don't smoke.

That's probably why."

"That's a lie," he said. "All inmates smoke."

"Not me, sir."

Then he started interrogating me. "Don't lie to me. Why does he call you 'college convict,' anyway? Those two words don't go together. You shouldn't be in prison if you've been in college. What's your charge? Why are you here?"

I had been incarcerated for a year at that point. A year later, and I was still having to explain why I was there, revive my nightmare, and prove my remorse. This was my reality.

"DUI manslaughter, sir."

The other officer knew my story already. You could tell he was tense and uncomfortable. He wanted the interrogation to stop, but he wasn't going to say anything. Officers stuck together. Right or wrong, they always stuck together.

Officer Smith continued to question me: "Who did you kill, convict? Whose family did you destroy? You ever think about what you did? You ended a life, inmate."

Trying to hold back my hurt, anger, and frustration, I could feel my fists tightening up and my heart racing. I had to keep my cool. The last thing I wanted was to be considered disrespectful and have this visit with my family taken from me. If I was "out of line," they would have punished me and sent my parents, who had driven two hours to see me, home.

"Every single day. She was my best friend. We first met when we were five years old. Not a day goes by that I don't wish it had been me instead."

He told me to "drop"—meaning I owed him 25 push-ups before I could go to visitation. This was summer in Florida. Just minutes before, I was excited and looking forward to visiting my parents. Instead I was sweating and holding back tears through push- ups on the hot pavement. When I finished, I asked for permission to recover (meaning I could stand up.) He ignored me for a few minutes before he finally said, "Carry on."

I looked him in the eye and said, "Is there anything else, *sir?*"

He said, "No." He granted me permission to carry on. I could finally go to visitation with my parents. As I started walking away, he shouted, "Double time!" He was ordering me to run. I was ordered to run across the prison compound to visit my parents.

When I arrived at visitation, I was visibly upset and sweating. My parents wanted to know what happened. Just then, the three officers from the hill walked into the officer's station of the visitation building. I think they wanted to see if I was going to say something to my parents, and I did. That was nothing new. My parents were no strangers to the stories I would tell them at visitation. Visitation was the only safe place to let them know about the corruption that was really happening behind the scenes. Why wouldn't I just tell them on the phone or in a letter? That wasn't an option, as calls were recorded and mail was reviewed. In prison, if you file a complaint about a staff member you are placed in confinement "under investigation" while they look into the matter. You're alone in a prison cell, unable to call your family or go to visitation. If I had complained about this officer, I would have been taken to confinement and forfeited the visit with my family that day.

It was never the inmates I worried about; it was the officers—you know, the people who are there to "maintain order." Unfortunately, not everyone knows how to check their baggage at the door. Some officers carry their personal problems, opinions, and biases to work with them. You never knew what to expect. Yes, prison inmates committed a crime.

Yes, they are there to serve their time. But it's the judge, not a corrections officer, who determines when they leave. No inmate should have to hear the words "if you ever want to leave here."

There were, however, a few officers who kept me going in the darkest of times. They were the angels looking out for me in that hellhole. They advised me of how to handle the most uncomfortable situations and reminded me of the impact I was making—no matter how small it felt. I don't know how I would have navigated prison without their counsel.

Watching *20/20*: Labels I Placed on Others

I was in prison when the *20/20* special finally aired on TV. I watched in a common room with a bunch of my peers. It's already weird enough having to watch somebody else's narration of your story on TV and the dramatization of it that Hollywood does, but having to watch it from prison surrounded by fellow inmates is something I just can't put into words. You're watching images and words of the life you used to live— your life before you walked through those gates into the prison—but you never know what the final outcome will be when you participate in major media. Just because you do an interview here and there, you don't know how they're going to piece that together. You don't know what the final product looks like. I was terrified to watch, but more so I was terrified for the officers and the fellow inmates to see it. *What are they going to think now? Will the women I am tutoring look at me differently? Will this change or affect the trust I built?* I felt so exposed, but I needed to know what was being put out into the world. I needed to see for myself.

The episode was nothing like I expected. There were pieces that were cut out, pieces that were used, and people who were interviewed who I had no idea would be on it. The thing that stuck out to me the most was that, throughout the entire special, was Rohom Khonsari, the state prosecutor for my case. He was doing his job. He was explaining why I should have gone to prison, he was explaining the statutes, he was defending the family. He was the same man whom I had always known—the prosecutor, the enemy—but something different happened at the end of the show. At the very end, *20/20* host Elizabeth Vargas turned to Rohom and asked, "Do you think Laura would want Jessica to go to prison?" He immediately responded, "Nobody can say what Laura would want, but I know what I would want." You could tell very clearly that he did not mean to say all of that. Elizabeth followed up with "What do you mean? What would you have wanted?" You could tell Rohom was just so uncomfortable. He had fallen into his response. He said, "I'm sitting here picturing my best friend right now, and I wouldn't want him to go to prison for a mistake like this." I couldn't believe he was saying that. For these years I had only looked at him as the enemy. He was the state prosecutor. He was the man who was on a mission to ruin my life. He was the enemy, and he saw me as the enemy as well. I thought he considered me a horrible person and that was all there was to it.

I had placed that label on him, just like everybody had placed a label on me. I never once considered that there was a person behind the prosecutor—that this was someone doing his job and that maybe, just maybe, this was something that kept him up at night. Maybe he didn't think I did this on purpose or that I was a horrible person, but maybe he thought I made a mistake. There was a human element there that I had never seen before. I was immediately overwhelmed by a feeling of guilt, thinking about how much pressure had been put on him through these years. How difficult must it have been to be the prosecutor on a case like mine? In these cases no one wins, no matter the outcome. By watching that *20/20* special, I was able to remove the label I had placed on him, and I started to see the person behind the prosecutor. Instantly, I was overwhelmed by a new level of guilt. I couldn't begin to imagine how difficult it must have been for everyone involved in this case, from the judge to the lawyers. I felt horrible for putting them through two and a half difficult years on the case because of my horrible decision to put the keys in the car ignition that night.

Starting Over

Nobody talks about coming home from prison. I never anticipated it would be so hard. It was the day that I had counted down to for four years and marked on my calendar. I felt like it would never come and then, when it finally did, I was terrified. *How much has changed in the world I knew? Are people going to accept me again? Who's really going to give me a chance? Who am I now? Have I changed? Has it been for the better or the worse?*

I felt like prison would be some kind of dirty film I couldn't scrub off and everybody would be able to see it. When I finally came home, I jokingly asked a friend, "How am I supposed to start dating? How would I even go about meeting someone? What am I supposed to say?" When she recommended that I sign up with a dating website, I thought she was crazy—because four years prior, that wasn't nearly as popular or common. I was convinced that was the way to meet a serial killer and I had just left prison a few weeks earlier. No, thank you. She assured me that this was normal and that everybody did it these days. If nothing else, it would be a big boost in confidence and it would get me used to having normal conversations again. I hesitated but went for it.

A guy named Chad messaged me and we hit it off right away. He felt like an old friend and he asked me to have dinner with him. I said yes, but the night we were supposed to go out I was ready to bail. I was working at a restaurant that night, and just as my shift was about to end, I walked into the bathroom to call Chad. I was terrified. What if we went out to dinner and he found out I had just come home from prison, and it was a big awkward mess? What if he left me right there in the restaurant? I didn't want any of that. I just wanted to lay it all out on the table and be transparent from the beginning.

So I dumped it all on him. I called Chad and said, "Look, I don't think I can go out with you tonight. I'm just going to give you the opportunity to bail." Then came the word vomit: "I just got out of prison. I'm out on probation. I've been gone for four years. I don't really need to be dating. This just isn't going to work for me. I don't want it to be this awkward situation." Then I briefly told him what happened. Surprisingly he was still on the phone. I had been certain he would have hung up by then. Instead he went on to tell me, "Look, you made a mistake that could have happened to any of us. That definitely could have happened to me before. You're lucky you're alive." And then he said, "I'll be there in 15 minutes to pick you up." I couldn't believe it.

Not only did he still want to go out with me, but now I was going to have to go out on a date with the guy that I just word vomited all over. The air was clear, but now Chad knew I was recently released from prison. Could there be a more awkward first date? (I'm going to guess the answer is no.) So there I was, even more nervous than I had been before I made the call.

Much to my surprise, everything went perfectly.

We sat at the restaurant lost in conversation with one another—so much so that, when we finally looked up from one another, we realized the restaurant staff were trying to close for the night. We were the only customers left. Clearly it was time to go.

By taking ownership of those fears and those concerns from the beginning, there were no hesitations, and we were able to speak openly without smoke and mirrors. He felt like an old friend I had known my whole life. He never passed judgment or asked weird questions, like I assumed he would. He allowed me to simply be in the moment and process this awkward social moment that I was slowly starting to ease into.

In the months following my return home from prison, I was having a really difficult time living in my parents' house. Don't get me wrong: I love my parents and my little sister, and I could have lived with them forever.

The problem was my bedroom. I was living in the same bedroom where Laura and I had sleepovers, the same bedroom where I spent two years with an open case, the room where I hid and where I was tormented by nightmares and flashbacks. I felt like those four walls were closing in on me yet again—as if, rather than taking a step forward with my life, I was taking 10 steps back, back into that place where I was before I was sentenced.

As difficult as I knew it would be, I had to step out on my own. I decided moving near downtown would be best, since I couldn't drive. That location would make it a lot easier for me to get around and find a job that I could easily get to. Chad decided to make the move with me. The first day we went job hunting, I walked into a beautiful restaurant in the perfect location. They were just opening their doors for the day, and I popped in to grab an application. Everyone was so friendly, and they excitedly told me to come back around 3:30 p.m. for an interview. Chad and I went and had lunch, and I filled out the application. At 3:30 on the dot, I was back at the restaurant for an interview. I couldn't miss the opportunity to meet management face to face.

Having an interview was so important because I knew my new reality: I had to check that dreaded box on the application that said "Yes, I've been convicted of a felony." I knew I was going to be looked at differently, and if my application went into a stack of papers with everyone else's, mine would be pushed to the side. When I walked back into the restaurant, a gentleman greeted me at the door and showed me to a booth, where we sat down to talk. This was unlike any job interview I had ever had. We sat down and, before he could say anything, the word vomit came out again. As he reached for my application on the table, I put my hand on top of the paper and I said, "Look—before you read this, I just want to talk. I'll be honest: I don't look very good on paper. There are some things in this application that may make you look at me different. . . ."

I told him my story and I assured him, "But if you give me a chance here,

I will appreciate that opportunity more than any employee you've ever had. I'm going to work harder than anyone on your staff. This would be a second chance for me and I will not let you down." He did not show any expression. He just sat there and listened the whole time. Then he said, "Are you done?" All I could think was that I had completely ruined this opportunity, but he was smiling, and he didn't address any of my word vomit. He went on to tell me that he was the owner of the restaurant and my heart sank. I was certain I just threw this job opportunity right out the window. As I sank down in my seat, he told me all about the business, their culture, why he started the restaurant, the heart behind it, and his vision for the future. When he was finished he asked, "Do you have any questions for me?" I said, "I don't think so, no."

He smirked and said, "Great! When do you want to start?"

"Can We Not Talk About It?"

I couldn't believe it. He was really going to give me a chance. I'm sure I said thank you a few hundred times before nearly skipping out the door. This opportunity was going to help me put the pieces back together.

Living and working in the same place, in the same city, in the same town was forever nerve-racking. When a customer would tell me that I looked familiar at the restaurant, my stomach would instantly knot up. *Do I know this person? Did they know Laura? Did they see me on TV? Do they recognize me? Are they thinking, "That's the girl from the accident?" or maybe I just look like someone they know?* Living in the same town meant quite a few people I knew came into the restaurant where I worked. I was embarrassed every time I saw a former classmate, someone I went to high school with—whether they knew Laura or not.

The pity stare crushed me, as did the small talk. "Hi. How are you? How have you been?" What was I supposed to say? "*Oh, awesome. You're a nurse? You are a paralegal? Wow, great. What have I been doing? Oh, you know, just getting out of prison. No big deal. Can I get you an appetizer to start?"* I wanted to run and hide in the back of the restaurant.

You never knew who was going to walk in. One of my first Friday nights at work, the pressure was on. I had to prove to the managers that I could handle this busy restaurant, that I could outwork others, and that I would show up in a big way.

Everything was going fine until I saw Rohom walk into the restaurant with his wife and another couple. In walked my former state prosecutor, the man who had spent two years of his career working toward putting me in prison.

He spotted me. I spotted him. As much as I wanted to run over and talk to him, I didn't want to ruin his night. Obviously, he was there on a double date with his wife. I didn't want to be the "crazy girl from that one case" who made a scene at their dinner. I took a few laps around the restaurant, walking by and looking over at their table. I had to say something. I needed him to know that I wasn't carrying a grudge against him. I felt horrible that I had put him through the turmoil I had during that case, and it wasn't until I saw *20/20* that I realized there really could be a person behind a prosecutor.

I walked up to their table and the small talk began. "How are you? How are you doing?" He introduced me to everyone and he said, "Let me go get a business card from the car. If there's ever anything I can do to help you, just let me know." He came back from his car and was standing at the edge of the table. He handed me his business card and went to shake my hand. Instead of shaking his hand, I gave him a hug. I said, "Look, I want you to know that I don't blame you for anything. I understand you were just doing your job. There's no hard feelings on my part."

Rohom was speechless. I'm sure it was the last thing he was expecting from me. I had been carrying so much weight for labeling him the enemy, and that weight had just been lifted.

Message: Labels Can Make or Break You

Murderer, drunk driver, broken, inmate, damaged, criminal, crook, crazy, medicated, unaffected, failure—the world placed a lot of labels on me. As much as I wanted to run and hide from it all, I couldn't. That wouldn't serve anyone else. If I wanted to help others, I needed to take ownership of it all: the good, the bad, and the ugly.

If I wanted to change the labels, it was up to me to do so—not the people who placed them on me. I needed to prove them wrong. Time, action, and consistency are the only things that can impact the way the world sees us. We may not be able to control how others view us, but we can do our best to influence their perspective.

But before we can influence others, we have to believe in ourselves. We have to look at ourselves through new eyes if we want others to do the same. Have you given yourself the time, action, and consistency to shift your own perspective?

Time: Change doesn't happen overnight. Give yourself the space (and grace) to just keep going. It may seem like the road is never-ending, but you're probably much closer to that new label than you realize.

Action: Doing what you've always done will leave you as you always have been. What actions can you take today that will put you one step closer to where you're striving to be? Keep taking action, even when you can't measure the impact.

Consistency: Anyone can try something new. It takes someone fully invested to commit to a new journey. When things get hard, keep going. When people question your motives, keep going. When it feels like you're not making as much progress as you hoped, keep going.

When you pause for a moment and look back on the time, action, and consistency you've put in, the labels that once existed don't look so relevant anymore.

Taking ownership of my actions (and labels) allowed me to stand my ground and say: *"Yes, this is what I've done but that is not who I am."* As a result, others began to view me in a new light and even with a new label: survivor.

Consider This

Is there a label that you placed on yourself (or that was placed on you) in the past?

What kind of power are you assigning to the labels others have placed on you?

When you revisit that label today, it does not accurately define you, does it? That's not the term/phrase you would you use to describe yourself. Rather than looking behind you, let's glance ahead. When you envision the good work you are going to do, the lives you are going to impact, and all that you have overcome, what do you see?

"My story helps others _____."

"I am paving the path for others to _____."

"_____ is/are impacted for the better by the work I do."

How can you take ownership of your life by creating a new label for yourself and the road ahead of you? What actions do you need to take to make that new label your reality?

Turn Your Mess into a Message

Let your story be the light that guides others out of their darkness.

Picking Up the Shattered Pieces

As I was starting to put the pieces of my life back together, it only made sense that I would go back to my university to finish school and get my degree. I hopped on the computer, I started looking at classes, and I picked out the perfect schedule, but the site wouldn't let me enroll in any of them. I thought this was quite odd, so I called the school. The admissions counselor initially told me, "No problem. Let me look it up for you." Then her tone changed. She was no longer excited and eager to help me enroll in school, but she had a very upset tone in her voice. It felt as if she didn't know how to say the words that she was about to tell me. She said, "I'm sorry, Ms. Rasdall. You're not allowed to enroll in school here." Puzzled, I replied, "What do you mean?" She said, "You violated the student code of conduct by being convicted of a felony."

Wow. I had no idea that when you've completed your sentence and served your time, and you try to go back to school to get your diploma, they'll tell you no. They'll tell you that you screwed up and you can't come back. It was gut-wrenching. Prior to my sentencing, I had shared my story and spoke to all of the incoming freshman at USF. But now that I had made it out the other side, I wasn't allowed back. The admissions counselor told me there was a loophole and that I could go in front of a board and appeal my case. But you know what? I was tired of explaining myself.

I was tired of having to appeal my case and tell my story and constantly be "the girl in the accident." I just wanted to be Jessica. I wanted to figure out who Jessica was and deliver something valuable to this world. I thought this degree was going to help me do that.

I figured out another loophole. I would enroll at St. Petersburg College, take a course first semester, and then transfer back to the university. That way, I wouldn't be a student who had violated the student code of conduct trying to re-enroll; rather I would be a transfer student. That didn't go as planned, either. I couldn't prove that I was a Florida resident to enroll in the school. Why? I'm not allowed to have a driver's license, so I didn't have that. I'm a convicted felon, so I can't vote, so I also didn't have a voter's ID. I didn't have a year's worth of utility bills or a lease because I hadn't been home from prison for a year. Although I had been a property of the state of Florida for the last four years of my life, I could not prove that I was a Florida resident.

Every time I tried to take a step in the right direction, it felt like there were 10 obstacles standing in my way saying "no, do not pass." At the time, I felt like everybody was just trying to stop me from doing the right thing, but looking back, I see it completely differently. There I was, trying to pick up all those broken pieces. I was trying to force them back together and somehow try to re-mold that thing I had shattered— the life I shattered. Instead, what I should have been doing, and what I ultimately did, was pick up those broken pieces and create something new—something different. There's no way to put the pieces back together. That path—that traditional path that I had been on (that of a college scholarship student)—and that girl were gone and broken. I had to carve out something new, but without knowing what that new thing was, it got scary.

I decided I would just keep working at the restaurant. I would try to stack up as much money as I could to get back on my feet, complete my probation, and figure out what was next in my life. Obviously, going back to school was more of a hurdle than I wanted to take on right then. When I really sat down to think about it, maybe that wasn't the best path for me. Yes, that was the traditional path. That was what everybody else did. I wasn't everybody else: I was a convicted felon. "Would a quality job require a degree, yet still hire a felon?" I questioned. Things just weren't adding up. Maybe this was a subtle message that I needed to shift in a different direction.

About a month after getting shut down on returning to school, the frustration faded and optimism settled back in. I began talking to my mentors and doing a bit of research. I knew I wanted to help others through difficult times. I wanted to help them create plans and pick up their pieces, but I didn't know what this would look like or even if that was possible. Obviously I couldn't be a therapist. It wasn't really the path I wanted to go down, nor was I mentally equipped for that. I didn't want people to come to me to solve their problems; I wanted to encourage them to face them head-on. This was when I was introduced to the idea of coaching and life coaching. *Okay, something that finally feels right.* Rather than trying to fight my way back into school, I decided I would invest in coach training. I would get this specialized training to help others in a new way.

I wasn't exactly sure where I was going with this coaching certification. I didn't know what this path looked like, but it felt right. It felt like I was taking steps in the right direction, and I wanted to keep going. I started working with female business owners to craft their difficult stories in a way that served others, yet still protected themselves. If there was one thing I had become really good at through these years, it was figuring out how to turn a mess into a message.

There I was, changing gears, creating a new path, but still feeling like the convicted felon who was always going to be stuck working in the restaurant. Would this work of helping others be able to fulfill my financial needs, or would this just be something I continued to do on the side while I worked at the restaurant?

When Katie Called

Two years after returning home from prison, I received a phone call from *Katie*, Katie Couric's show. A producer wanted to talk to me about an upcoming special. That was certainly unexpected.

I had been hiding under a rock and hadn't been doing as much speaking, as I was trying to figure out how to start my life over, though quietly behind the scenes I was still speaking at some substance abuse centers and teen driving programs. The call from Katie Couric's producer was completely different than any other media phone call I had received.

Every interview before had been hyper-sensationalized, and it felt like they were trying to paint me like a monster. They had always been focused on opposing views and making the story as dramatic as possible. This producer explained that they were putting together a redemption episode.

They wanted to highlight my story not because of the damage I had done, but because of the steps I took afterward—because I tried to make it right. How did these people see that? I was still having a hard time seeing that in myself and they saw it. I still hesitated a little bit to say yes, because doing anything with the media is scary and I didn't know if I wanted life after prison to involve that.

Do I just want to run and hide from this, or am I forever going to be the girl in the accident? This would be my first media experience in front of a live studio audience. It was an opportunity to share my voice, in my own words, and to let people see what was really happening behind the scenes. I said yes, and *Katie* flew Chad and me to New York for filming.

When we walked into the green room, we met the other people being interviewed on this episode. We had no idea who was going to be on the show. (They don't tell you that ahead of time.)

Inside the green room were three people, one of whom was Todd Bridges, the TV star from *Diff'rent Strokes*. What was I doing there? Did I really fit in this mold? Here was a TV star from the 1980s and me, the girl who killed her best friend. I was starting to get a little worried about the perception of the show, but we sat behind the scenes at a table watching Todd's interview on the screens in the green room, and it was genuine. Katie Couric asked him some questions about where things went wrong, but not many. The focus was what he did next. How had things changed in his life to overcome the adversity? To right the wrongs that he had done? That's where the focus was. This started to put my nerves at ease a little bit, because I had never been in an interview like that. Those I had done previously tended to be confrontational in trying to paint me as a monster. This was going to be very different.

As we sat watching the recording in the green room, Chad and I started chatting with the other two people in there. (Thankfully, Chad was with me while I waited to go be interviewed by Katie Couric, and he was there to help and keep me calm and support me every step of the way.) The man and woman who were in the green room with us seemed to be getting along very well. Maybe they were old friends? They clearly knew each other but as we started talking to each other and asking what brought us to the show, their story was unlike anything I had ever heard: The gentleman had robbed and shot the woman, and left her for dead. Somehow by the grace of God she survived and forgave him, and they were able to move on with their lives.

Throughout this whole journey, stories of powerful, earth-shattering forgiveness—like this one—had been placed in front of me, and every time I hear one a range of emotions is triggered. First, I always think, *Wow, I could never do that. Would I be able to forgive like that? Could I put myself in his shoes?* The second thing I think is: *I wonder if there will ever be forgiveness like that for me? I wonder if things will ever change with Laura's family? I wonder if some of the friends I've lost along the way will ever look at me differently? I wonder what it must feel like to know that you've been forgiven.* I can't help but believe there's a reason these stories keep getting placed in front of me. They give me hope to keep going, and they're a gentle reminder that even if we forgive people along the way we're not ready to say that to them directly.

Watching this man and woman share their story of forgiveness and redemption stunned me. Two people from once-opposing sides had come together to do great work and serve a bigger purpose. I was in awe of their strength. When it was finally my time on set with Katie I was terrified. I was so nervous. These people had powerful stories and I stood: the murderer. I wondered, *Who am I to be on a redemption special?*

As Katie asked questions and I told her the story, it was difficult to be open with her. This interview was so different than the others. Before, I felt like I needed to hold back in order to protect myself. This time, it was as if I needed to hold back to protect her. I could see the tears welling up in her eyes, and a part of me wanted to stop. Maybe this story was too much. I didn't want her to hurt or anyone else. I couldn't bear to see another person upset. When the cameras turned off she told me that she wished every young adult could hear my story—that every teenager would have access to this. She looked at me like a human, not a monster, as other reporters had. That episode and that media experience changed the dialogue that had been told before. I was no longer the "Drunk Driver Killed Eckerd College Student." I was now simply the woman trying to keep her friend's memory alive and prevent others from repeating her mistake.

A New Life

A few weeks after returning home from filming Katie Couric's show, I found out that I was pregnant with my daughter. In flooded all of the emotions. I was terrified. I was nearing the end of my probation, and I couldn't help but wonder, *How am I ever going to provide a life that this little girl deserves as this felon?*

I was excited to be a mom, and as soon as that excitement hit, it was followed by guilt, the kind of guilt that just crushes your chest. *Who am I to bring life into this world, when I have taken one out? Who am I to raise a human being when I am silently struggling to make it through the day?* I had taken away someone's daughter, someone's sister. How on Earth was I allowed to be a mother? I feared for the life ahead of her—what people would say. *Will kids on the playground be cruel? Will she forever live her life in the shadows of my mistakes?*

I wanted to protect this little baby from everything and everyone, but I didn't know how.

Over the years, Laura had been that quiet voice in my head, that underlying motivation that kept me pushing through the darkest of times. She was the reason I kept going, the reason I faced everything I did, and the reason I made it out the other side. When we do things solely for ourselves, it's easy to give up. It's easy to throw in the towel when it gets hard and say, "I'm not good enough" or "I don't deserve this."

But when we're doing it for someone else, something bigger than ourselves, we don't want to let them down. Who was I to let Laura down? Who was I to stop, or quit, or give up, when she never had the chance to start? I wasn't going to do that. When my daughter was born, I had a whole new level of motivation and fight. It wasn't just Laura anymore. It was the two of them. The life I was living and the work I was doing weren't just to provide for myself, but to provide for my daughter, to create a life that she could be proud of, and to be that example.

Throughout the entire pregnancy, I wanted to run and hide and not be the girl in the accident anymore. But once my daughter was finally here, I just wanted to make her proud. I knew that stopping these presentations was not even an option. I had to keep speaking. I had to keep inspiring others and letting people know that yes, you can make it through the darkest of times. You can take horrible situations and find the good in them. You can serve others, even when you feel you're not worthy.

But how? *How am I going to do that? How am I ever going to go and travel and reach the masses, if I am stuck working in a restaurant?* It was time to get serious about creating a life that would allow me to serve in a bigger way.

Thankfully, Chad believed in me more than I ever believed in myself. On the days when I wanted to give up, or didn't think I was good enough or that I deserved it, he was the voice in my face, not just in my ear, reminding me, "You have worked so hard for this, and you're making a difference. You can't stop now." He supported every crazy dream and backed all of my plans. He filled the role in my life that was once held by Laura. He's my best friend. He acts as a mirror when I can't see my own worth. We all need someone like that in our life—someone who will be our sounding board, support us on the journey, and remind us why we started when things get rough. My parents have supported me every step of this journey, but a part of me always felt as though they "had to" since I'm their daughter. Having support from someone outside of your immediate family helps you feel validated in the darkest of times.

I decided I was going to dive head-first into coaching, and help more women than I ever had before. But I had to revisit my presentations. I couldn't keep giving the talk of the girl in the accident. There was so much more there. There was a bigger message of inspiration and survival and rewriting your life story.

Just as I started to get into my own message, I received another phone call from a TV producer.

One Bad Choice

It was a producer who called me a year earlier. They had been working on a new TV show that would be called *One Bad Choice*. The last time she had called, she asked me to participate in the pilot episode, which I politely turned down. It didn't make sense for me to go through the emotional turmoil of filming something that may never impact a life. What if the pilot was never picked up?

This time, she was calling to let me know the pilot had been picked up by a major TV network, and they still wanted me to be a part of it. She said,

"MTV has picked up our show, and we want your story for the drinking and driving episode." I quickly said, "Again, no thank you." MTV is huge, and I was in an in-between space of wanting to run from the identity of "the girl in the accident" and wanting to go "all in." I was terrified to say yes. But just as I told her no, she shared a personal story with me.

First she said that I needed to consider the target market: "MTV reaches ages 15–24, and that's exactly who needs to hear this message. They need to hear it from someone who has been in their shoes and they can easily relate to." She reminded me that doing this would allow me to impact more lives than I ever had before, really make a difference, and keep Laura's memory alive. I said, "Why my story?" Unfortunately, this happens across the country every single day. There are countless stories of teens who experienced drinking and driving fatality.

She then explained the real reason she wanted my story on the show. Through tears, she told me her brother was killed by a drunk driver. Until she heard my story, she carried so much anger and hate at the person who took his life. She said, "When I saw your story and realized what you go through every day and how this has impacted your life, it made me look at the driver in my brother's case differently. I never once considered the pain that this caused him or the guilt he lives with every day. You've helped me forgive the man who killed my brother."

Her words stopped me dead in my tracks. That was never something that I intended to do. That was something I didn't even know was possible. We set out on these missions to share a message and impact lives, but we never know how big that ripple effect is going to be, what people will take from it, or the difference we will ultimately make.

That producer gave me hope that not only could I prevent others from repeating my mistake and inspire them to overcome their own mistakes, but maybe I could even bring people to forgiveness. She changed my entire perspective on the work that I was doing, and I agreed to move forward with the show.

Participating in the MTV show was unlike anything I had done before. This time, there was no interview. It was me telling my story and then actors re-enacting it. I was terrified. I was terrified of watching my story like an outsider.

As much as I knew I would get to tell my story, I had learned from my past media experiences that you never know how it will be edited and cut. But here, the reward outweighed the risk. If I could impact just one of the lives this show would reach, it was worth the pain, the emotional distress, and the backlash I would experience.

The message behind the show was to let young adults realize we're not invincible and that it only takes one bad decision to shatter everything— to throw it all away. The silver lining, though, was that the show also captured what these young adults had done after their failures.

The producers and film crew came with me to one of my speaking events. They came to my home and met my family. They wanted to see the reality behind the scenes. What had I done with my life? How was I still making an impact? And for them, getting to see the reaction from the students in my presentation was priceless. That allowed them to see firsthand the difference this story was making and ultimately the impact the finished show would have.

We finished filming, and then it was back to the day-to-day life of coaching my clients and raising my daughter. The show wouldn't air for nearly a year after recording, so I nearly forgot about it. That is, until I received a text message from a friend: "I just saw an MTV commercial with you in it. Your story is the series premiere for a new show?? How did I not know this?" I hadn't told many people about the show, and I honestly wasn't ready for it to air. I had been under the radar for a few years and the criticism had slowed. The last thing I wanted was for the harassment to come back, especially now with my daughter in my life. I didn't want her to experience the aftermath of my mistake.

I wasn't ready for my story to be so public again. I wasn't ready to watch my story be re-enacted by actresses. I wasn't ready for the positive feedback, or the backlash and criticism. I was terrified of the final product and how they might spin my story, as some other outlets had done.

I wanted it all to go away, but it was too late to back out.

What will everyone think? I had created a new life as a mother, a business owner, and a soon-to-be wife. So many people in my new life didn't know much about the accident. They didn't know much about my story. Yeah, maybe they knew I was in an accident, and maybe some even knew I went to prison, but that's it. Now, my whole story was going to be rehashed and re-enacted. What would they think? *Will they look at me the same way?*

The one person who I was most nervous to have watch the show was my little sister. I had kept so much of this from Catalina. Now she would not only see the whole story, but she would see it re-enacted. She was in high school when it aired and I knew it was important for her to see. I wanted her to watch it. I wanted her friends to watch it. I wanted everyone to learn from my mistake. *But will they look at me differently? Will they be able to look at me at all?*

As the show came on, I had the biggest knot in my stomach, my hands were sweating, and my voice was trembling. But it wasn't as bad as I thought. The two actresses who played Laura and me didn't really look like us. The first half of the show embellished my story a bit to make for a more appealing a TV show. It felt less like my story and more like I was watching a TV drama.

The second half of the show—now that was more difficult to watch.

The second half of the show didn't have the actresses in it. It was me, my new life, and my new family. The world was being shown a side of me they had never seen before. I was watching my story unfold in a way I had never seen.

I wasn't just "the girl in the accident" anymore. I was the girl who had made it out the other side and committed to do something good. This girl had an amazing family backing her up—a new family she would sacrifice anything for. This woman was doing amazing work and serving her clients like she never dreamed she could. This woman was still speaking, still raising awareness, and still keeping Laura's memory alive. This girl had turned her mess into a message.

Watching this show confirmed for me that these two different people could be put together into one. The girl before the accident, the awareness she raised, the good work she was doing, the mom, the business owner—these roles could all go hand in hand. Before, it had felt like two completely different worlds. The duality of it all was playing out right before my eyes.

Yes, I could provide the life my family deserved and still do good work. It had been nearly four years since I returned home from prison. I was nearing the point where I had been home longer than I was incarcerated. This perspective fired me up. Life was too short to drag my feet. I poured into my business, and I continued to speak at schools. My speaking calendar was quickly filling up when I received a phone call from one of the last people I expected: Rohom. He asked if I had time to meet him for lunch that week, as he wanted to discuss something with me.

We met for coffee and he told me how proud he was of me—proud that even after serving my time in prison, coming home, and struggling to start a new life, I had still continued to speak and raise awareness. I couldn't believe what I was hearing. Just a few years prior, everyone (including Rohom) was convinced my motive for speaking was to get out of serving a prison sentence. I didn't blame them. In fact, had I been on the outside looking in, I probably would have questioned my motives as well. But my continued efforts and current-day actions allowed the truth to shine through. My heart was in the right place, and it always had been. The rest of the world was starting to see that.

Rohom saw the impact I was making and he asked if he could help. My former state prosecutor was offering to speak alongside me. I couldn't believe it. How powerful it would be to step onto a stage, and tell my story, and then introduce the man whose job it was to put me in prison. This would not only show teens the reality of being the offender, but it would also show them what they would be up against if they repeated my mistake. Rohom could shine a new light on what the legal ramifications really look like.

I knew I would never have the story of forgiveness, like Bruce or John. I knew I would never be sharing the stage with Laura's family. But when I thought about the impact Rohom and I could have together, I knew it would be as close as I had ever gotten or would ever get to that.

I reached out to the upcoming speaking events that were booked on my calendar and asked if Rohom could share the stage with me. We spoke together and shared this message, in front of the U.S. Navy, a mock DUI event, and multiple high schools.

As I began to talk about the prosecutor who put me in prison, I told the audience, "I can't put words in his mouth, but I'm sure that it wasn't an easy job that he had to do. So, rather than make any assumptions, I'm going to let him tell you his side of the story." As Rohom stepped onto the stage, you could hear the audience gasping for air as they tried to figure out what was going on. Certainly, this couldn't be real—but it was.

Message: Ditch Your Plan for the Path

The life the "Old Jessica" planned and the future she envisioned were nothing compared to the life that I had been called to lead or the things that would be placed in front of me. The good work that I would do and the lives that I would impact? Those were never part of my plan. At the end of the day, it's really not about us at all. It's not always our plans that matter, but the path we're on.

There are amazing things that we are here to do. There are lives that we are here to impact, and some of these roadblocks, hurdles, and things we just don't understand are put in front of us to guide us down a different path. It may feel like a detour, but sometimes that detour is going to land you exactly where you're supposed to be. My friend, the impact you're going to have is so much bigger than you ever dreamed of.

What Can I Do?

Define your mission that serves a purpose bigger than yourself. When things get difficult, it's easy to give up or to throw in the towel when our work only serves ourselves. If we're clear on who our mission is serving, it's much more difficult to give up in fear of letting others down.

Who are you serving, and how does your mission impact them?

What actions or activities can you do to reach them?

Once you've defined the path you're heading down, be flexible in how you round each curve. I knew that my mission was to keep Laura's memory alive and prevent others from repeating my mistake. My plan involved me speaking and sharing my message, not media exposure. At first, I resisted these opportunities because they were not a part of my plan. Sharing my story through the media allowed me to reach more lives than I could have on my own.

When you're faced with a detour, rather than immediately saying no, ask yourself if this new route still serves your greater purpose.

CONCLUSION:
I'm Still Rewriting My Story

Eleven and a half years after the accident, and I'm still rewriting my story.

I'd like to think that Laura would be proud of the path I've chosen and the work I've done. The wounds haven't healed. I'm not sure they ever will, but you can learn how to navigate the pain in ways that serve others.

I have a box in my closet (and always will). The box contains Laura's necklace that I wore the night of the accident, her clothes that were left at my house, pictures of our childhood together, and questions of who she'd be today. The box also houses my hospital ID bracelet and inmate ID card, which remind me of the journey after the joy ended.

Although the criticism has slowed since I returned home from prison, it certainly hasn't stopped. As I sit here writing these final words to you, I'm terrified to put this book on bookstore shelves. I'm terrified of the backlash that awaits me. I'm terrified to fall back into the role of "the girl in the accident." I'm dreading rehashing and reliving the darkest days, and opening the door to uncomfortable conversations.

As I was wrapping up the final touches on this book, I snuck away to a hotel to write for a few days. I don't drive, so I called Lyft to have a driver to bring me to the hotel. My driver was an older gentleman, and I could immediately tell that he was a man of faith from his mission trip t-shirt and the Christian station playing on the radio.

I hadn't told him my story at all but we started to talk about the book and how, particularly when we go through difficult times, people often pressure us to seek forgiveness. But what about those moments when we're not able to hear "I forgive you"? What if there's a sudden loss? Do we throw in the towel? Do we stop working toward healing if we can't hear the words "You're forgiven" or "I forgive you"?

We cannot let our progress be determined by words that come out of someone else's mouth. That's an uncontrollable factor. If we go through something difficult, someone does us wrong, or we make a mistake, does not hearing the words "I forgive you" mean we can't take the next step? Does that we can't move forward or start our own journey of healing? Does that mean we shouldn't do the next best thing or serve others? Absolutely not.

My Lyft driver was a little upset about this. He began to tell me about the power of forgiveness, and I quickly realized I hadn't given him enough context. I told him my story.

"I wanted nothing but to hear the words 'I forgive you,' but that was something that I could never hear. I was never going to hear those words. Did that mean that I would just stop? Was the accident where everything would end? I wasn't sure why I survived, but I believe I was called to serve in a way I had not before. I want to inspire others to keep going. When you're in a moment of darkness and you don't see the light at the end of the tunnel, you're losing hope and you're not going to hear 'I forgive you. You're forgiven,' what do we do next?"

He suddenly seemed more at ease and said, "Okay. I get where you're going with this now." He began to tell me a story about a young man who spoke at his church. "This young man went the wrong way on the interstate. He went up the off ramp, and he hit a young girl head-on and killed her. This girl was related to my pastor."

Shocked, I interrupted him: "Do you mean John? Are you talking about John?"

I told the driver, "I cannot believe you're talking about John right now. It is such a small world. Our fathers ran cross-country together in high school. He's the one who gave me hope in the darkest of days. John may not know this, but when I was in the hardest part of my own healing after my journey and my accident, he was that beacon of hope for me. He was the light at my end of the tunnel. He let me know that people can go through these difficult things, and make it out the other side and do amazing things with their life. John has traveled across the country speaking and now runs a recovery center on the beach. He is leaving a bigger impact on this world than he knows."

Out of my own mouth came exactly what I needed to hear: *He gave me hope in the darkest of days.* I was supposed to be in the car with that Lyft driver. The process of writing this book has allowed doubt to resurface. The days of questioning "Who am I to do this?" have been plentiful.

Writing this book wasn't about me at all. Why was I allowing my fears and doubts to get in the way? This book could be that beacon of hope for someone else. These words could inspire someone in the trenches, like John did for me.

What are the chances that I would get into that particular car and have that particular conversation? It's not chance. Pay close attention to the people who are placed in your life. Whatever it is you need to hear, see, or know, there will be people along the way to remind you of what's possible and what you're truly capable of.

You never know who you're inspiring with the work you do. You never know how many years down the road it's still going to impact them. When you're doing the hard work, you're not always able to see the impact. But you cannot calculate how many lives you're changing, the difference that you're making, and how long that impact is going to last. Have faith and know that you are making a difference, and keep doing it anyway.

Sometimes the "good" in my life is still too much to bear and I feel unworthy of it all. There are still mornings when Chad has to comfort me from traumatizing nightmares.

There may be a long road still ahead of me, but when I glance in the rearview mirror, I can't help but believe that after the worst mistake imaginable, I took the next best step. Laura has continued to leave her mark on this world in ways that I never imagined were possible.

Sometime in your life, something big will shatter. You won't be able to piece it back together. But you are always able to pick up the pieces and make something new out of what remains.

About the Author

When Jessica Rasdall was a freshman in college, she made a life-altering decision that resulted in the death of her best friend. With her life, as well as so many others, shattered, Jessica went to a bookstore in search of a self-help book, and couldn't find any that she could relate to.

She started to pick up the pieces, to try to make something out of what was left. In an effort to raise awareness, cope with her guilt, and keep her friend's memory alive, she began sharing her story with high school students across the country. It was then that she discovered the power of storytelling. In their faces she saw them relate to personal tragedies and mistakes, but she also saw hope and willpower. She connected with her audience in ways she never anticipated. She saw change. And she knew she had to keep telling her story. Jessica spoke to more than 15,000 young adults across the country before she was sentenced to prison.

Today, Jessica Rasdall continues to share her story of turning her "mess into a message" as a motivational speaker and public speaking strategist. She partners with business owners to craft stories and presentations that connect with their own audiences. By rewriting their stories, her clients are transforming what were once considered limitations into some of their greatest business assets.

Jessica has been featured on major international media outlets such as ABC's *20/20, Katie, The Guardian, MTV,* and many more. She has spoken to hundreds of high schools and universities as well as business conferences, major organizations, and even the United States Navy.

You can learn more about Jessica and her speaking presentations at www.JessicaRasdall.com.

96420792R00064

Made in the USA
Lexington, KY
21 August 2018